Kaspar Hauser

Where Did He Come From?

Kaspar Hauser

Where Did He Come From?

A phenomenological inquiry into
Rudolf Steiner's question

by

Terry Boardman

Illustrations by David Newbatt

**Wynstones
Press**

Published by

Wynstones Press
Ruskin Glass Centre
Wollaston Road
Stourbridge
West Midlands DY8 4HE
England

Telephone: +44 (0) 1384 399455
Fax: +44 (0) 1384 399463
Email: info@wynstonespress.com

Website: www.wynstonespress.com

First Edition: 2006

© Copyright Terry M Boardman and David Newbatt, 2006

British Library CIP Data available.

ISBN 0 946206 60 0

Printed in EU by Cambrian Printers

Contents

Preface   7

Introduction   9

Chapter 1: Rudolf Steiner's Comments about Kaspar Hauser   11

Chapter 2: The Element of Place in the Incarnation of Kaspar Hauser   16
    Southern Germany   16
    Swabia and Baden   19
    Schloss Beuggen   26
    Nuremberg   28

Chapter 3: The Element of Place in the Incarnation of Kaspar Hauser
    – Conclusions   32

Chapter 4: The Element of Time in the Incarnation of Kaspar Hauser   36
    The Age of Materialism   36
    The Christ Rhythm in History   38
    Crossing the Threshold of the Physical World: 1780-1781   39
    The Massacre of the Innocents   46
    Mars and Mercury   47
    Napoleon   49
    The NAROS cycle   52

Chapter 5: Enemies and Allies   56
    Kaspar Hauser's Enemies: Groups   56
    Kaspar Hauser's Enemies: Individuals   62
    Summary   92
    Kaspar Hauser's Allies Beyond Nuremberg   94

Chapter 6: Kaspar Hauser's Life:
    Its Sevenfold Rhyth and Historical Consequences   124

Chapter 7: Conclusion: Kaspar's Spiritual Origins   132

Endnotes   168

Index   175

index of Names   182

Preface

This book is to be understood only as thoughts that serve as a modest supplement to the far greater work of Peter Tradowsky on the subject of Kaspar Hauser. It offers some thoughts that seek to complement at a lower octave what Peter Tradowsky has given in his wonderfully inspiring work *Kaspar Hauser - the Struggle for the Spirit* (Temple Lodge, 1997). It will proceed from more exoteric considerations in the first half to more esoteric ones in the second. The book is an extension of a talk given to the English-Welsh Regional Conference of the Camphill movement at Trigonos Residential Education Centre in North Wales, April 2004. All royalties from the sale of the book will go to the Camphill Foundation, which receives donations for further work with people with special neeeds who live in Camphill Communities.

I would like to thank the Camphill Community for giving me the opportunity to present the talk and immerse myself once again in this profound and moving subject. In particular, my thanks go to Vivian Griffiths, Susanne Pickering and Susanne Steffen for their initiative and encouragement that made the talk and then this book possible. I would also like to thank Mark and Rosalind Gartner for all their support, friendship and insights over the years.

Terry Boardman, Christmas 2005

Introduction

When Bruno S. is on-screen, it's impossible to tear your eyes away from his one-of-a-kind performance, but Herzog wisely gives a spare but eloquent context for "The Mystery of Kaspar Hauser." An anatomical dissection of Kaspar Hauser is quickly carried out, revealing nothing but our eagerness to search for answers, even when they're wrong. In contrast, Herzog shows us the landscapes that surround his story, recreating the lush colour experiments of photographers of the mid-nineteenth century. Herzog's anachronistic images and Bruno S's newly-reborn eyes make more sense of the mystery than all the state-of-the-art scientific bumbling of 1833 or 1993.[1]

Although, according to Masson (writing in 1996), there have been more than 3000 books and at least 14,000 articles written on Kaspar Hauser, the mystery still seems as far as ever from being solved.[2]

Some people would prefer to keep Kaspar Hauser as a mystery. They would prefer the truth about him not to be understood so that he would remain a pathetic example of a feral child, a psychological oddity. He is perhaps best known in the English-speaking world through Werner Herzog's cynically titled 1974 film *Every Man for Himself and God against All* (English language title: *The Enigma of Kaspar Hauser*), which sees him in just this sense of a lost innocent abused by a cruel world. "In the end, all attempts at civilization prove to be nothing more than a crushing of the human spirit, and Kaspar Hauser sinks into the sanctity of his bed, delusional – regressing to his primeval soul, lost in his dreams - a broken man."[3] This essay is more concerned to draw back the veil on that 'mystery,' as it is the writer's conviction that the story of Kaspar

Hauser is of tremendous significance for the modern age and calls out to be understood.

In the last month of his life, as he lay on his sickbed in the Schreinerei (carpenters' workshop) near the ruin of the First Goetheanum Building, on 3rd March 1925, Rudolf Steiner, founder of the spiritual science of Anthroposophy, spoke to his pupil Ludwig Polzer-Hoditz of three great issues in history that anthroposophists should busy themselves with: the question of the two Johns – John the Baptist and John the Evangelist; the identity of Dmitri, the would-be young Czar of Russia at the turn of the 16th century; and thirdly, the question: **Where did Kaspar Hauser come from?** The particular turn of phrase seems significant here – not, *Who was Kaspar Hauser?* but, *Where did he come from?* Not in terms so much of his inheritance and his genetic line, but rather, *What was his spiritual origin?* In connection with this are the following words of Rudolf Steiner, given to Ludwig Polzer-Hoditz on the same occasion:

> *It is not a question of who Demetrius [Dmitri] was, who Kaspar Hauser was, but of what was to have been achieved by them. One should occupy oneself with the question as to what was to have been brought about by them, for by such a direction of investigation we shall always gain the key to an understanding of many problems.*[4]

It is this question that I would like to address in this contribution to the theme of Kaspar Hauser. As I am not a clairvoyant, I would like to do it by looking at certain phenomena of space and time in his earthly life and trying to see if they give us any clues as to his spiritual origin. I will therefore approach the question not directly from the spiritual centre, as it were, but rather from the periphery and work in towards an answer from there.

Chapter 1

Rudolf Steiner's Comments about Kaspar Hauser

First, let us recall what Rudolf Steiner himself had to say about Kaspar Hauser. Peter Tradowsky in the above-mentioned book cites all the known comments of Rudolf Steiner about Kaspar Hauser. For instance, Steiner described him as a *"stray Atlantean, a straggler from Atlantis,"* [5] thus pointing back to Kaspar Hauser's connection with Atlantis, a time when spiritual beings, angels and demons walked the earth. The Bible has a memory of this in Genesis, Chapter 6, when it speaks of "sons of God" and "giants." Rudolf Steiner, whose principal task was research into reincarnation and karma, said that he could find no previous incarnation of the Kaspar Hauser individuality on earth and also no subsequent incarnation after 1833. [6] We can thus deduce that in Atlantis the Kaspar Hauser individuality was not in fact a human being; it was not a human incarnation, but an angelic one. At this point it should be noted that Kaspar Hauser's 19th century incarnation was very much connected to that of Napoleon, who had adopted the girl who would be Kaspar Hauser's mother, Stephanie de Beauharnais, and had arranged her marriage to Kaspar Hauser's father, Karl von Zähringen, later the Grand Duke of Baden. Rudolf Steiner said that he had not been able to find Napoleon's previous incarnation either, but that he had been "a Mars spirit," one for whom the sojourn in the spiritual sphere of Mars between death and a new birth had been especially important. Napoleon had, moreover, "forgotten his mission." We can speculate that his mission may have been to work with the French Folk Spirit in such a way as to facilitate a peaceful confederation of Europe or at least, a more fruitful cooperation of European nation states, though given the strength of resistance of the conservative and traditional forces in Europe at that time, it is difficult to see how he could have achieved this by political means; perhaps commerce and industry – the application of iron in other ways – might have been a more suitable vehicle for him. As it was, Napoleon chose instead to make himself Emperor of the French, a people who were of course mostly descended from the Franks, that ancient Germanic tribe who had a very strong connection with the Niebelungs. The name Niebelungs again reminds us of Atlantis, for it means "mist" (Nebel, in German), and the atmosphere of Atlantis, according to Rudolf Steiner, was permanently swathed in mist; nothing had sharp daylight contours there. Like Napoleon's inner being, Atlantis was a veritable mist-ery.

Rudolf Steiner implied in June 1924 that *Kaspar Hauser had been an angelic being,* and that is precisely what he apparently then went on to call him in September 1924 during the course of lectures he gave to the Christian Community priests. In notes made by Ludwig Polzer-Hoditz on 3rd March 1925, Steiner said that Kaspar Hauser "*worked into the Rosicrucian connection from the beginning* [and had an] ...*important esoteric mission for Christianity.*" This is a very significant indication. "From the very beginning..." – when was that? Of course, one could say that it was in the Sun Oracle on Atlantis, but in post-Atlantean times, it may have been in the 4th century AD, when the individuality who had not long before been incarnate as Mani, (216-276) the founder of Manichaeism, called a great council in the region of the spiritual world above Colchis in modern Georgia, attended by the spirits of Zoroaster, Gautama Buddha, and Skythianos. At this meeting, the three of them, representing the highest forces of thinking, feeling, and willing respec-tively, and inspired by Mani, laid the seeds for what, 1000 years later, would become the first earthly development of Rosicrucianism, when the youth who would later incarnate as Christian Rosenkreutz was initiated. Mani himself, who, according to Rudolf Steiner, appeared by Christ's side at the time of Golgotha as the Young Man of Nain, would go on to incarnate in the 9th century as the Ego Bearer Parsifal. Just after 1250, a highly significant date that Rudolf Steiner related back to the midpoint of the Atlantean epoch and spoke of as a particular time of darkness for humanity,[7] was a time when the overwhelming Mongol forces, with their decadent shamanistic and backward-looking Luciferic wisdom that was Turanian-Atlantean in origin, were threatening to completely overrun the West. The combined military forces of Europe were shattered by the Mongols at the Battle of Liegnitz in modern Poland in 1241. It was at this time that the individuality of Christian Rosenkreutz was initiated by 12 representatives into all the wisdom of the Atlantean and Post-Atlantean epochs up to that time. It is noteworthy that Rudolf Steiner specifically refers to the one of the 12 who carried the wisdom of the Mars sphere. 1250 was, after all, the time when Samael, the Mars Archangel was the ruling Time Regent (1170-1510). The one to be initiated took in all this wisdom of the twelve, and then 'died,' aged just 20, but his soul almost instantly returned and rayed back to the 12 their own accumulated wisdom, but in a metamorphosed manner that spoke of the Christ Event. He then died and did not return to earthly incarnation for approximately 120 years, not until 1378. This was Christian Rosenkreutz, who then lived on Earth until 1484. In the case of Mani as the Youth of Nain and again as Parsifal the Fool, and now here with the initiation of Christian Rosenkreutz, we have a new impulse coming through *a youth*.

The Kaspar Hauser individuality then, was most likely associated with Rosicrucianism from its very beginnings in the 4th century, with the council called by Mani, and most probably with Mani himself, which is of course not to say he *was* Mani himself, as Kaspar Hauser had no previous incarnations before 1812, according to Rudolf Steiner's research, whereas in the case of Mani, we know of at least seven, one of whom was one of the three Magi, Caspar – traditionally shown as a dark-skinned North African – whose gift to the Jesus Child was myrrh, symbol of death and resurrection.[8] Mani was reborn as the Youth of Nain, the Son of the Widow, and the first to be raised from the dead by Christ. After his next incarnation as Parsifal, the pure fool and later King of the Grail, who brought to the Grail his half-brother and former enemy Fierifis, he then initiated Christian Rosenkreutz (the Lazarus-John individuality) again in 1459.[9] It is worth mentioning in passing that Rudolf Steiner said that Charles IV, who reigned from 1349 to 1378, was the last initiated Holy Roman Emperor of Germany; interestingly, Christian Rosenkreutz was reborn in the same year, 1378. Mani's teaching was deeply concerned with the Mystery of Good and Evil, Light and Dark, and it is above all in this realm of spiritual activity, in his capacity to absorb evil and yet bring transforming light, that we shall see the angelic being, the Kaspar Hauser individuality, unfolding itself in the 19th century incarnation as Kaspar Hauser. Mani was born into the Persian culture, and into Manicheism flowed much of the wisdom of the second Post-Atlantean epoch – the struggle between the Sun-Being Ahura-Mazdao and Ahriman, the Spirit of Lies and Materialism. This struggle was also a key feature of the period of Kaspar Hauser's life between 1812 and 1833. In the roof of the large cupola in the First Goetheanum, Rudolf Steiner portrayed what he called the Persian-German Initiate, reaching toward a child figure and between them the word "ICH." The I is born out of darkness and shines like an invincible flame within it, illuminating it.

> I gaze into the darkness
> In it arises Light
> Living Light
> Who is this Light in the darkness?
> It is I myself in my reality
> This reality of the I
> Enters not into my earthly life;
> I am but a picture of it.
> But I shall find it again
> When, with goodwill for the Spirit
> I shall have passed through the Gate of Death.[10]

Karl Heyer, an anthroposophical historian, recorded that Rudolf Steiner said of Kaspar Hauser that *"alongside Christian Rosenkreutz, he was the one who most understood the sufferings of Christ,"* but Heyer notes that this statement is not well-authenticated. What is well-authenticated, however, is that Rudolf Steiner also made the astonishing remark that *"If Kaspar Hauser had not lived and died as he did, all contact between earth and the heavenly world would have been completely severed."* Now this must make us think. Usually, anthroposophists just take it literally and think that when Steiner says 'the earth' here, he means 'the whole world.' But there are many places in his lectures where it is quite clear that when he says 'mankind' or 'the world' or 'Man,' he actually means 'Europe' or 'European humanity.' This is not a question of some kind of racism; it was simply normal for people in his day to speak in such a way. We can ask ourselves therefore, whether here too, when he says: "...all contact between earth and the heavenly world...," he may actually have meant "all contact between *Europe, or western civilisation* and the heavenly world would have been completely severed," because, arguably, it was not uniformly throughout the world, but in Europe (notably Britain, then in the first throes of the Industrial Revolution) above all, where the darkness of materialism was reaching a peak during Kaspar Hauser's lifetime 1812-33. We can see, for example, that there were contacts between "the heavenly world" and other regions of the world during that time. For instance, the new spiritual stream of the Baha'i developed between 1819 and 1844, interestingly, in Persia. And in Japan, the new syncretistic faith of Tenrikyo began with the revelations of its founder Miki Nakayama in 1838, just 5 years after the death of Kaspar Hauser. The United States too saw a number of new evangelical and charismatic movements emerge in the first third of the 19th century. Nevertheless, Rudolf Steiner's formulation should give us pause for thought: "...if Kaspar Hauser had *not lived and died as he did,* all contact ...would have been completely severed." This seems to imply that there was a degree of inevitability to the manner of Kaspar Hauser's life and death – that he had to suffer in that prison, that he had to be murdered. In other words, it implies a *sacrificial* life – and death. This is hard to contemplate, given the awful circumstances of that life and death. This theme of sacrifice will be considered in more detail later in this essay when it will become clear that in fact Kaspar Hauser's sacrifice was indeed for the whole world and not just for the West.

Chapter 2

The Element of Place in the Incarnation of Kaspar Hauser

I would like to turn now to some phenomena of the places in Kaspar Hauser's short earthly life. This will entail a number of digressions from the subject of Kaspar Hauser himself, but I trust the reader will come to see how these are all related to him and to the question of his origin, for we are trying to see how the phenomena surrounding his life shed light on his mission and his spiritual origin.

Southern Germany

In 1555, half a century before the Rosicrucians were heard of in Europe, the Provençal astrologer Nostradamus wrote:

> *A new sect of Philosophers shall arise,*
> *Despising death, gold, honours and riches,*
> ***They shall be near the mountains of Germany,*** [emphasis TMB]
> *They shall have abundance of others to support and follow them.*

The stage on which Kaspar Hauser's life unfolded was entirely in southern Germany, beginning in the southwest. On the Rhine, between Germany and France, and bordering on Alsace-Lorraine, itself a region of great esoteric and exoteric significance in the history of Europe, was the dukedom of Baden and its capital of Karlsruhe (meaning: Karl's rest), where Kaspar Hauser, the rightful Grand Duke of Baden, was born on

Michaelmas Day, 29th September 1812. It is a fact of no small interest that **a direct line on the map of Central Europe connects *Karls*ruhe, where Kaspar was born, Ansbach, where he died, Nuremberg, where he appeared, and *Karls*tejn Castle** (Karl's stone, today Karlstejn, just west of Prague), built to house the Imperial Crown jewels by the Holy Roman Emperor Charles IV (1349-1378), who was the last such ruler to be initiated into the mysteries of esotericism. Today, Baden forms part of the German federal state of Baden-Württemberg, the richest state in Germany, with its capital in Stuttgart. Not far from Karlsruhe, and also in the same dukedom, is the old university city and cultural centre of Heidelberg, which was the focus of the Rosicrucian movement of the 17th century around the court of Frederick of the Palatinate and his English wife Elizabeth Stuart, daughter of King James I (1603-1625). In pre-Christian times, this area of Baden along the east bank of the Rhine, which includes the Black Forest, would have formed part of the area of influence of the Hibernian mysteries. Opposite, on the west bank of the Rhine is the Odilienberg (Mont Ste Odile), itself built, according to Rudolf Steiner, in this area of the Hibernian mysteries, which stemmed ultimately from the Sun Oracle of Atlantis.

During the time of the migrations of the Germanic tribes c.300-600 AD, this area of south-western Germany was settled by the Alemanni and Suevi tribes. In 868 it would have formed part of the kingdom of Lotharingia (Lorraine), which encompassed a long stretch of territory that included modern-day Holland and Belgium down through the Rhineland, Burgundy, Switzerland (including Dornach) and much of northern Italy as far as Rome. This long but narrow multi-ethnic kingdom, ruled by Lothar, one of the sons of Louis the Pious and grandson of Charlemagne, was sandwiched between the land of the Franks to the west and the lands of the Germans to the east. In 869 it ceased to exist when it was invaded by both Charles the Bald, King of the Franks (French) and Ludwig, King of the Germans. It shrank to a rump in northern Italy, and thus began the histories of the three territories that would eventually become modern France, Germany, and Italy. The later small region of Lorraine, together with neighbouring Alsace, would several times play a decisive part in determining the destinies not just of France and Germany but of all Europe. Today, the European Parliament meets in the Alsatian city of Strasbourg on the Rhine, where Goethe studied, close by the Odilienberg and not far from Karlsruhe. Walter Johannes Stein, one of Rudolf Steiner's closest pupils, writes in his book, *The Ninth Century and the Holy Grail*[11] that "most of the ruling families of Europe were of the race of Odilia."[12]

That same year 869 was commented on by Rudolf Steiner on innumerable occasions as the year of the 8th Council of Constantinople, when, as he put it, "the spirit was abolished" and the human trichotomy of body, soul and spirit was reduced to a dichotomy of body and soul – a seemingly obscure theological event that was to have the most profound consequences for all future European development. The destruction of the middle kingdom of Lotharingia in 869 was the political correlate to this event, while in the spiritual world, the meeting took place between the individualities that had been Alexander the Great and Aristotle on the one hand and Harun al-Rashid and his counsellor (Steiner implies it was Jafar Barmakid, but his father Yahya, a very wise man, seems more likely in view of Rudolf Steiner's continuous references to Harun's wise counsellor) on the other. Meanwhile, in this same momentous year, Steiner tells us, occurred the meeting in the etheric realm of the earth between the two streams of Christianity – the *etheric* Christian stream proceeding from the Hibernian west, that is, the pre-Christian Arthurian and Druidic stream that had foreseen the coming of Christ as He descended through the etheric realm of the Earth, and the *astral* Christian stream proceeding from the east – the Grail stream carried in the hearts of those who had actually experienced the Events of Palestine on Earth and in the hearts of their followers and successors. Finally, working from indications given by Rudolf Steiner, his pupil, Walter Johannes Stein in his book *The Ninth Century and the Holy Grail*, indicated that three important years related to the events of the Grail stories themselves, 823, 828, and 834. The story of St Odile in the mid-7th century around 666 is also very much bound up with the Grail events of the 9th century and of 869. Indeed, Rudolf Steiner indicated that the anti-Christian impulses of 666 led directly to the

Council of Constantinople in 869. This has to do with the Anti-Christ Sun Demon's assault on the Middle. Within the human being, the middle term has always been expressed in western esotericism by the principle of mercury, or quicksilver, that which, in Rosicrucian alchemical parlance, is able to relate the two poles of salt (head – thinking) and sulphur (metabolism – will).

In looking at this corner of Germany, we are led back to the first half of the 9th century, the time of Charlemagne and the founding of the Holy Roman Empire of the German Nation, as it came to be called. This empire, which was born in 800, was finally destroyed a thousand years later in 1806 by Napoleon, who fancied himself and his family as its successors. Whereas Pope Leo III had crowned Charlemagne Holy Roman Emperor on Christmas Day 800, Napoleon placed the imperial crown of the French Empire on his own head in 1804; the Pope was present at Napoleon's coronation but relegated to the role of an onlooker. A thousand years of German history thus came to an end in 1806 as the West, in the shape of France, attempted to dominate Germany and central Europe completely. It was as part of this strategy of harnessing Germany to France that Napoleon had in the year of the dissolution of the old German Empire, arranged the marriage of his adopted daughter Stephanie Beauharnais (adopted in the same year) to Karl of Baden; six years later Kaspar Hauser would be born to this couple. The family name of Stephanie, who was the instrument chosen for this harnessing, was Beauharnais, which means 'beautiful harness.'

Swabia and Baden

In the early Middle Ages, much of Switzerland, as well as Alsace-Lorraine and Baden, was part of the medieval duchy of Swabia (the name comes from that of the Suevii tribes), which also included the town of Basel and its environs. The Alsatian dialect stems from old Alemannic. To assuage the ambitions of Rudolf I, King of Burgundy, the King of Germany, Henry I, severed Basel from Swabia in the 10th century and gave it to Burgundy. In gratitude, Rudolf presented Henry with an artefact recovered from Italy – the Holy Lance, an important symbol of the inheritance of Constantine. This supreme relic was said to be the lance with which the Roman soldier Longinus had pierced the side of Christ at the Crucifixion.

The family of Kaspar Hauser's father originated in Zäheringen, near Freiburg, which is also close to Basel and Dornach. Many of the great names of German history – Hohenstaufen (Fredrick I Barbarossa and Fredrick II were of this dynasty), Zähringen, Habsburg (which later provided so many of the emperors of Austria) and Hohenzollern (later the royal then imperial Prussian dynasty) – are all place names in Swabia. From Hohenstaufen in particular came mediaeval Germany's greatest kings, at whose courts flourished the culture of the *minnesänger,* as well as Wolfram von Eschenbach, Walther von der Vogelweide, and Gottfried von Strassburg. It was in this milieu that the *Niebelungenlied* and the German Grail stories emerged. After the collapse of the political power of the Hohenstaufen dynasty in the mid-13th century, the power of the duchy of Swabia faded. But the sense of Swabia as a cultural region did not die, and in 1376, two years before the birth of Christian Rosenkreutz (1378-1484), 14 cities banded together in the Swabian League of Cities, which grew to include over 32 cities from Basel in the west to Regensburg in the east, and from Constance in the south to Nuremberg in the North. It was from Nuremberg in 1356 that Emperor Charles IV issued the famous Golden Bull which determined the political constitution of the Holy Roman Empire until its dissolution in 1806, six years before Kaspar's birth, and confirmed the principle of the election of the Emperor by seven princely Electors. It could be said that the Golden Bull did more than any other single formal political measure to prevent Germany developing into a single-nation state of the type that would emerge in Western Europe. It ensured that the middle region of Europe would not be a solid unitary state like either France or England, but rather a more fluid and variegated collection of political entities – in short, it ensured that Germany's political form would be more <u>mercurial</u> in nature. It was the last initiated Holy Roman Emperor, Charles IV, who issued the Golden Bull and he did so in the south-eastern German city that would forever be associated with the names both of Kaspar Hauser – and Adolf Hitler. *This southern region of Germany – from Karlsruhe to Beuggen, near Freiberg and then to Nuremberg/Ansbach – is the whole area in which Kaspar Hauser lived his earthly life.* In 1488, a new alliance, the 'Swabian League' was formed by the cities of south Germany. In the 16th century, the Holy Roman Empire began to organize around the administrative unit of the Kreis, ('circle') and the southern German states called themselves the Swabian Kreis.

A mediaeval story circulating in Germany was known as 'The Richest Prince.' It was later set to music composed by Justinus Kerner and regarded as the Württemberg anthem. It indicates something of how Swabia has been viewed in Germany as an area particularly rich in a social spirit:

1st verse: An assembly of German princes once sat down in the Grand Hall in Worms to praise the value and achievement of their kingdoms with fine words.

2nd verse: The Prince of Saxony spoke up: "Wondrous is my kingdom and its power, its mountains conceal a wealth of silver, although it is buried deep down."

3rd verse: "Look at the sumptuous wealth of my kingdom," spoke up the Elector of the Rhineland, "Golden crops in the valleys and wine on the hillsides."

4th verse: "Grand cities and rich monasteries" spoke up Ludwig, Ruler of Bavaria, "make my kingdom just as rich in treasures as yours."

5th verse: Eberhard the bearded one, the much-loved ruler of Württemberg, spoke up: "My State is one of small towns, and has no mountains laden with silver."

6th verse: "But it does conceal a precious jewel: In the forests, no matter how big, I can lay my head in perfect trust in the lap of any one of my subjects."

7th verse: And the lords of Saxony, Bavaria and the Rhine cried out: "Bearded one, you are indeed the wealthiest of all; your kingdom bears a treasure of untold value!"

The city of Karlsruhe (Karl's rest) is quite young compared to other German cities. A hundred years before the three year-old Kaspar was taken away from it, margrave Karl Wilhelm founded it in 1715 because he wanted to have a palace where he could rest after hunting in the nearby Hardtwald forest. Having decided to establish a town around the palace, he attracted immigrants from all over Central Europe to Karlsruhe because he granted them many benefits: no taxes were due for twenty years; they were given free land and wood, and religious freedom was guaranteed. The late Sun King Louis XIV of France was the trendsetter in those days, and Karl Wilhelm saw himself too as the sun of his state and built his new capital with streets radiating out like sunbeams from the palace. The city was thus associated from its founding with images of the sun and peace.

However, it is noteworthy that the principal areas of Kaspar Hauser's life – Baden, Karlsruhe, Nuremberg – were all historically Protestant, and that the Rosicrucian movement of the early 17th century strongly identified itself with the spirit of the anti-Papal Reformation.

The early years of the Reformation saw a dynastic and political division in Baden in 1535, which brought about the emergence of two smaller states, Baden-Baden, ruled by a Catholic family, and Baden-Durlach, ruled by an Evangelical family. Karl Friedrich (1738-1811), Kaspar Hauser's paternal great grandfather, reunited Baden in 1771 and inaugurated countless reforms in the spirit of Enlightened Despotism. In alliance with France, he achieved the expansion of Baden from 3600 square kilometres with about 175,000 inhabitants in 1803 to 15,000 square kilometres and almost a million inhabitants in 1810.

The new Grand Duchy of Baden (after the dissolution of the Empire in 1806) received a new government and administrative organization and in 1810, land reform based on the French model. The constitution of 1818 and elective legislature were models for early German constitutionalism. **The lower chamber was virtually a school for the Liberal-Nationalist movement.** In 1831, the year of Hegel's death and two years before Kaspar Hauser was murdered, a wave of sympathy and support for the Polish rebellion against Imperial Russia and its attempt to re-establish a free and united Poland swept through Germany. On 22nd March 1832 Goethe died and on 27th May, approximately 30,000 people, many of them students, gathered at the Hambacher Fest in the Palatinate to voice their demands for a liberal, unified Germany, for freedom of the press, for the lifting of feudal burdens, for religious tolerance – and even, as demands grew bolder and more radical, for the proclamation of a republic. Predictably, a wave of arrests followed, as well as new laws to suppress liberals. The 1848 Revolution in Germany began on the 27th February (Rudolf Steiner's birthday, 1861) in Mannheim, where a *Badische Volksversammlung* (assembly of the people of Baden) adopted a resolution. Mannheim was where Kaspar Hauser's mother, Grand Duchess Stephanie, had lived since her husband's death in 1818.

In April and September of 1848 Baden rose in rebellion under the leadership of the Left (F. Hecker, G. Struve) and in May 1849, with the installation of a republican regime, there was a revolution, which the authorities were only able to put down by calling on Prussian troops for assistance. After the period of reaction, the 'New Era,' 1860-1866, brought an attempt to form a liberal, parliamentary regime. In 1866 Baden turned back to constitutional ways under Friedrich I (1856-1907) and Friedrich II (1907-18), who reigned with the benefit of Nationalist and Liberal support. [13]

During the Revolution of 1848 Baden was the most liberal German state, providing twenty-six of the fifty-one liberal delegates to the Frankfurt all-German Parliament. The Revolution having started in Baden, it was also in Baden that the last revolutionaries were crushed by Prussian soldiers in 1849. The final revolutionary uprising, in Dresden (Saxony), collapsed on 9th May after a six-day battle, but democrats and republicans in the Palatinate and Baden fought on and were joined by almost all the regular troops of the Grand Duke of Baden. The Prussian crown prince Wilhelm (later Emperor Wilhelm I of Germany in 1871) marched to Baden at the head of 50,000 troops in June and suppressed the radicals in Baden with much violence. Here we see the signature: Prussia, representative of the old conservative autocracy, crushes Baden, the hope of the new liberal spirit. In 1833 it was Prince Metternich of autocratic Austria in collaboration with England's Lord Stanhope that brought about the frustration of Kaspar Hauser's mission; in 1848, Kaspar's land of Baden, where even without him progressive hopes faded only slowly, was laid low by reactionary Prussia. But German liberalism and the progressive spirit were not yet completely dead. The liberal Emperor of Germany, Frederick III, who tragically ruled for only 99 days in 1888, was married to Princess Victoria of Great Britain, eldest daughter of Prince Albert and Queen Victoria. Almost 250 years after the fateful marriage of the German Prince Frederick V of the Palatinate to the British princess Elizabeth Stuart, it was another disaster for relations between Britain and Germany that the liberal Frederick III and his Queen Victoria did not rule longer. His untimely death made the immature and unruly Wilhelm II Kaiser; Wilhelm and his uncle Prince Albert Edward of Wales, later King Edward VII, loathed each other. Frederick III's sister married Frederick I, Duke of Baden, whose nephew, Max von Baden, was made the last imperial chancellor of Germany by Kaiser Wilhelm II. Max von Baden came from the line of the family that had supplanted Kaspar Hauser's line through the crime of the Countess von Hochberg, the second wife of Grand Duke Karl Friedrich.

Thus it was not only on a prince of Baden, indirectly related to Kaspar Hauser, that Rudolf Steiner placed his hopes of bringing about the idea of the Threefold Social Order in 1918, but it was also on the direct descendant of the very woman who had had Kaspar Hauser abducted – the Countess Hochberg, Prince Max's great grandmother. Steiner met Max von Baden in Karlsruhe 20/21 January 1918, discussed the Threefold Social Order with him and passed on to him a copy of his lectures on *The Mission of the Folk Souls*.[14] It is noteworthy that US President Woodrow Wilson had formulated his 14 Points together with his *eminence grise* Col. E.M. House earlier that month (4-5th January 1918) and had announced them to the world in a speech to Congress on 8th January. Steiner intended that the Threefold Social Order should be Central Europe's answer to the world view encapsulated in the 14 Points. It would thus, in a sense, have been sounded into the world *from Baden.*

Steiner again met Max von Baden, who was politically a moderate, later in the year (date uncertain, but probably in late September or early October; von Baden became Imperial Chancellor on 3rd October – ironically, since 1990, 3rd October has been Germany's national day, the day of reunification) and no doubt pressed upon him the central significance of the Threefold Social Order ideas. Hans Kühn recorded that Rudolf Steiner expected

> *the new Imperial Chancellor to find the appropriate words, that is, to have the courage to proclaim straightaway to the German people in his inaugural speech, before the announced revolution took place [exactly 70 years after the 1848 revolution! – TMB] the idea of the Threefold Commonwealth as proof of a profound change and wish for peace of the German nation. Rudolf Steiner was very anxious to learn about the text of the inaugural speech when he got hold of the newspaper. Never afterwards did I see Rudolf Steiner so shattered as by this disappointment, which signified the defeat and path of suffering for the German nation. The Prince was unable to carry out the task assigned him by destiny. He subscribed far rather to the thoughts of Woodrow Wilson about the 'future happiness of nations.'* [15]

Von Baden announced his acceptance of the 14 Points on 5th October, two days after becoming Chancellor. On 9th November he proclaimed the abdication of the Kaiser and the end of the monarchy and resigned the following day, handing his office over to Friedrich Ebert, another native of Baden. In February 1919 Ebert was chosen to be the first President of the new Weimar Republic. In a lecture on 21st April 1919, Rudolf Steiner says: "...for those who look more deeply there was the disappointment that to the external military capitulation, the spiritual capitulation of Germany came about through the man [Prince Max] who many had seen as the last hope just in those autumn days of 1918." [16]

It seems that, along with other members of his family, Max von Baden recognised that Kaspar Hauser had been the legitimate heir to the throne of Baden, and Karl Heyer quotes in his book on Kaspar Hauser the French researcher and diplomat Edmond Bapst, who mentioned that Max von Baden had promised in 1913 to bury the remains of Kaspar Hauser in the ducal tomb in Pforzheim as soon as he would formally succeed to the throne of Baden. However, he never became Grand Duke, and died on 9th November 1929, 11 years to the day after he had proclaimed the end of the German Empire.[17] The 9th November has been a significant date for Germany on other occasions: Hitler attempted his Munich putsch on 9th November 1923; *Kristallnacht,* the Nazis' attacks against the Jews took place on 9th November 1938, and the Berlin Wall came down on 9th November 1989.

Schloss Beuggen

Kaspar Hauser was born in the region that saw the rise of the Rosicrucian movement in the 17th century and which was a centre of a liberal progressive spirit in Germany for many decades after the fall of Napoleon. After being kept for just over two years in the Karlsruhe area, he was transferred some time in 1815 to Beuggen Castle, Rheinfelden, on the River Rhine near Basel,[18] where he was kept until at least October 1816, when a mysterious letter in a bottle thrown into the Rhine at Laufenburg revealed that someone important was being held secretly in the area; Kaspar was then moved from Beuggen. In the autumn of 2002 I visited Beuggen Castle, which in 1815 had been a personal possession of the Countess von Hochberg of the House of Baden since the fateful year of 1806 (see above). I saw the recently discovered (December 2001) cellar room in which Kaspar Hauser had been kept as a child of under three years old. It had just one narrow slit of the old mediaeval castle arrow slit type in the wall looking out over the River Rhine some dozen metres below. From the outside it seemed that wooden slats may have covered over the slit, making it invisible and denying light to the cellar room. On the wall of the room facing the river was a small pathetic picture of a horse in a faded red colour; the picture has been dated to the early 19th century. Two wooden horses and a wooden dog were, we know, the only toys that the infant Kaspar had to play with during his early years. I noted from the inscription above the main outer doorway that the building in which Kaspar was kept had been built in 1666 – the number of the Beast thus literally upon it.

The castle itself had been a commandery of the Teutonic Knights from 1268 until the end of the Order in 1809, when Napoleon abolished the Order throughout his domains. The Order had been organised as such by Duke Fredrich of Swabia in the 1190's during the Third Crusade. Beuggen Castle was built in 1268 just after the defeat and execution of 16-year-old Conradin, Duke of Swabia and last of the Hohenstaufen Emperors of Germany. The interior walls of the castle chapel were decorated throughout with the skull and crossbones motif that was common in several of the crusading orders, including the Knights Templar. With the destruction of the Templars, the skull and crossbones motif was gradually taken over by various freemasonic groups and sinister forces, later becoming the symbol of Caribbean pirates as the Jolly Roger as well as the *Totenkopf,* death's head, of the SS and also the symbol of the pseudo-Masonic secret society at Yale University to which George W. Bush and his father both belong – Skull and Bones, founded in the USA in 1832-1833, the last year of Kaspar Hauser's life, allegedly as a branch of a German secret society by Yale men who had studied in Germany in the early 1830's.

The origins of Beuggen Castle thus point back to the High Middle Ages, the time when the Grail stories were popularised and when the German Emperors were struggling against the spiritual dominance of the Papacy. They recall the crusading orders, the Templars and the origins of Freemasonry. A skull and crossbones motif in damascene was found on the blade of the knife that killed Kaspar Hauser.[19] Most gruesome of all was the fact that the infant was incarcerated in a castle which, during the wars of liberation against his mother's stepfather Napoleon (1813-1815), had been used as a field hospital by the Austrian army and where some 3000 soldiers had died of typhus and been buried in a mass grave not 500 metres from the room where Kaspar Hauser was kept. The locals' fear of an epidemic meant that apart from his jailer and female governess Anna Dalbonne, no-one else lived at the castle when Hauser was there. What kind of people would keep a young child in such a place? In 1820 the castle became a children's home founded by two Swiss Pietists, Christian Friedrich Spittler und Christian Heinrich Zeller, who were influenced by the ideas of Pestalozzi. It continued as a children's home until 1981 when it became the seminar and conference centre run by the Evangelical church which it still is today.

Nuremberg

One of the facts beyond dispute in the mysterious story of Kaspar Hauser is that he appeared in Nuremberg in the Kingdom of Bavaria at 4 pm on Whit Monday, 26th May 1828. After Beuggen, he was imprisoned for 12 years – a Jupiter cycle. In esoteric terms Europe is especially associated with Jupiter, and Kaspar was known already in his lifetime as 'the Child of Europe.' It is thought he was kept for most of the 12 years of his imprisonment at Schloss Pilsach, a large house near Nuremberg. Pilsach was then owned by Mayor Karl von Griesenbeck (1787-1868), a mostly absentee landlord whose career took off spectacularly in 1817, his royal master the King of Bavaria himself becoming godfather to Griesenbeck's second son.[20]

Nuremberg is a city that arguably sits at the crossroads of Europe and which was an ancient trading centre that connected the Baltic and the Mediterranean, Iberia and Russia. Whitsun of course is a festival of light – the light of the Holy Spirit, of the holy tongues of fire that descended upon the Apostles at Pentecost. This was the spiritual fire of a new social impulse that enabled the apostles to speak to all people in ways they could understand – the fire of a social light in the darkness of the age.

When Kaspar appeared in 1828, Bavaria had already been locked in dispute with Baden since the Congress of Vienna (1814-1815) over ownership of the county of Spenheim in the Rhenish Palatinate, which included the cities of Heidelberg and Mannheim. This territory had been

taken from Bavaria by Napoleon and given to Baden. It was not given back at the Congress of Vienna, and its return became the near life-long obsession of Crown Prince Ludwig of Bavaria (King 1825-1848), Griesenbeck's royal master, who had spent his childhood in the area. Kaspar was caught up in this bitter territorial dispute over a region that has played such a fateful role in the history of Germany. Somehow (as yet unclarified), control over the infant prince passed from Baden to Bavaria in 1816-1817, and the Bavarians sought to keep him for possible future use in the struggle against Baden.

Kaspar Hauser appeared in Unschlittplatz in Nuremberg. The name, appropriately enough, means Tallow Square or Candlewax Square, and Kaspar was himself bringing a great light into the darkness of 19th century Europe as it approached the trough of its philosophical materialism. Halley's Comet, always the bearer of materialistic impulses, was looming; the comet would come closest to earth in 1835/6. Subsequent returns were in 1910 and 1986. Rudolf Steiner dated the beginning of "the war in heaven" – the Michaelic spirits' battle against the ahrimanic forces in the Moon sphere – to 1840-1841: some 4-5 years after the appearance of the comet. Kaspar Hauser thus appeared in Nuremberg 13 years before the beginning of this mighty struggle. After similar intervals of 4 years after the appearance of Halley's Comet, the First World War began in 1914 and the Gulf Crisis and War occurred in 1990-1901. Exactly one hundred years after the extinguishing of the candle of Kaspar Hauser in 1833 and the seeming failure of his mission, a very different voice was heard in Nuremberg thundering out its message of hate throughout Europe by the power of electricity, microphones, loudspeakers and radio. Nuremberg, the crossroads city of Europe was decorated with the *hakenkreuz,* the crooked cross, ancient symbol of the Sun that in all probability has its origin in the sun wheel designs of the Sun Oracle of Atlantis. It is a symbol now and forever enmeshed and entangled by Hitler in red blood and black soil. Napoleon, Kaspar Hauser, Adolf Hitler – were these all powerful Atlantean spirits? Nuremberg, the city that witnessed the presence of the pure messenger of Christ, Kaspar Hauser, became the centre from which the human instrument of the Anti-Christ announced the presence of *his* master. Were Napoleon and Hitler not in some way connected with decadent Atlantean impulses of priest-kingship and shamanistic symbolic magic? Did these two impulses, before and after Kaspar Hauser, not threaten to erase the spirituality of Central Europe and the message of its bearer – Kaspar Hauser?

Chapter 3

The Element of Place in the Incarnation of Kaspar Hauser – Conclusions

All the above phenomena relating to the principal places in Kaspar Hauser's earthly life suggest that his mission lay in a historical context of the most profound significance for the spiritual and cultural development, especially of Germany, and of Central Europe and Europe as a whole. The region in which he lived out his short life has been deeply connected with pre-Christian Mysteries, the origins of Germany as a social and political entity, with the events of the Grail story, with the Rosicrucian movement and with the Classical and Romantic movements of 1750-1850.

According to Ludwig Polzer-Hoditz, Rudolf Steiner said that:

> *South Germany should have become the new Grail Castle of the new Knights of the Grail and the cradle of future events. This spiritual ground had been well-prepared by all those personalities whom we know of as Goethe, Schiller, Hölderlin, Herder and others [notably Hegel – TMB]. Kaspar Hauser was to have gathered around him, as it were, all that existed in this spiritual ground thus prepared. But that was not wanted by those circles (the western lodges and the Jesuits). They could not tolerate a centre that was awakening to consciousness if they were not to relinquish their power and designs for power. A spirit such as Goethe's frightened them.*[21]

It is not difficult to see the truth of Rudolf Steiner's words when one considers the trio of King Ludwig II of Bavaria (1864-1886), Richard

Wagner (1813-1883) and Friedrich Nietzsche (1844-1900). Ludwig's palaces and castles, especially the miraculous Neuschwanstein, (New Swan Stone), conceived of as 'the Lohengrin Castle,' were clearly intended, as was Wagner's operatic citadel of Bayreuth, to be an artistic reflection worthy of the Grail Centre in South Germany. The entire interior design and decoration of Neuschwanstein Castle is devoted to the themes of Wagner's operas, climaxing in the decoration of the Great Hall, which is dedicated to the story of Parsifal. One can experience a feeling of real pathos when one reads the story of these three individualities – Ludwig, Wagner, and Nietzsche – and their relationships and realises that the lives of all three were somehow frustrated by the absence of one who could have supported and inspired them in their artistic and philosophical explorations. Kaspar Hauser as Prince of Baden would surely have smoothed away the ugly sides of Wagner's character – his prejudices, arrogance and anti-Semitism; Nietzsche would not have fallen into madness because he would have seen that idealism was far from dead in Germany, and that there was an alternative monarchical conception available to the country other than that of the Prussian dominated Reich, which Nietzsche castigated as responsible for the "extirpation of the German spirit;" Kaspar would have kept Ludwig's feet on the ground, and would have been able to do this because, at the height of his own powers, aged 36, he would have been able to make the most of the situation of 1848. He, rather than the reactionary Frederick William IV of Prussia, could have been the one offered the crown of Germany by the Frankfurt Parliament with its many representatives from liberal Baden. He then could have helped bring about the reconciliation of those other two great spirits, Ferdinand Lassalle, the Prussian Jewish labour leader who was not tempted by the fury of revolutionaries, and Otto von Bismarck, the action man and guardian of the past who was yet searching for a new Christianity. Lassalle and Bismarck clearly felt drawn together anyway, even without Kaspar Hauser, for they did communicate productively in a series of letters in 1863-1864. It was through the influence of Lassalle that Bismarck introduced the world's first system of social welfare measures. Unfortunately, Lassalle was killed in 1864 in a duel over a woman, and his negotiations with Bismarck were thus cut short. In 1878, 14 years after Lassalle's death, Bismarck spoke of him with deep respect in a speech to the Reichstag, as a very likeable and capable man from whom a great deal could be learned. Kaspar Hauser could have helped the two men to work together for social healing and a new constitution in German-speaking Central Europe.

Surprisingly, Bismarck was very sympathetic towards the architectual dreamer, Ludwig II, with whom he also corresponded. He recognised astutely that Ludwig's own family were trying to bring down the King. They were concerned that the building projects would ruin the ancient Wittelsbach family. Their materialism was short-sighted; today, Ludwig's castles and palaces attract millions of tourists and euros to Bavaria! But then the obsession of Ludwig's grandfather – Ludwig I (1825-1848) – with regaining the Palatinate from Baden had played a major part in the tragedy of Kaspar Hauser. One of the main reasons why Ludwig II retreated into his world of architectural dreams was because, after the defeat by Bismarck of Ludwig's ally Austria in the Austro-Prussian War of 1866, Bavaria was very much under Prussian control, and the King's freedom of manoeuvre was severely restricted. Prussia's victory over Austria conclusively terminated the debate that had been going on since the 1830s between the two competing visions of Germany, the idea of *kleindeutschland* or *grossdeutschland,* that is, respectively, a 'small Germany' without Austria and dominated by Prussia, or a 'big Germany' that would have taken in at least the German-speaking parts of the Austrian Empire and maybe the non-German-speaking parts too to form a Central European Federation. Without Kaspar Hauser to restrain and temper him, and after Lassalle's premature death, Bismarck, the man of action and will, allowed himself to be guided by 'blood and iron.' A worship of power, military and industrial, both influenced by and jealous of Great Britain, grew inexorably in Germany.

All this, and the tragic destiny of Germany and Europe in the coming decades, could have been forestalled had Kaspar Hauser lived to rule as rightful Prince of Baden. Guiding and tempering Bismarck and Lassalle, and inspiring the artistic trio of Ludwig, Wagner, and Nietzsche, as well as the all-German Parliament at the political centre at Frankfurt, Kaspar Hauser, from his base in the new Grail Centre in southern Germany, would have been at the heart of mighty endeavours that could have been healthily rooted in German-speaking Central Europe. The southern Germans, with their more affable, social, inward and mystical tendencies, had an affinity to the Spiritual, or Consciousness Soul, whereas the northern Germans were more at home in the Intellectual-Mind Soul and looked more out into the external world. So many threads reach out from Kaspar Hauser through the phenomena of place both to the past and the future of Central Europe. His sacrifice signified that a connection with the spiritual world could at least be maintained through the dark period of the nadir of European civilisation from 1841-1879. His earthly 'success' would have meant that the destiny of Germany and Central Europe would have been quite different from the deepening darkness of the years 1879-1945. Clearly, these phenomena of place in the incarnation of Kaspar Hauser point to a spiritual origin that is related to the hierarchical rank of the archangels, those beings who guide the destinies of social groups, communities and nations.

Chapter 4

The Element of Time in the Incarnation of Kaspar Hauser

Having considered the phenomena of place in the earthly life of Kaspar Hauser, and seen how significant these were to his relationship to the German-speaking area of Central Europe in particular, the phenomena of his time, of his historical era, should now be examined. Here again, we shall have to make some seemingly wide detours from the subject of Kaspar Hauser, but ultimately, it should be clear how all of this complex background necessarily provided the spiritual atmosphere in which his mission was set.

The Age of Materialism

As has already been indicated, during the years of Kaspar Hauser's earthly life and indeed in the period when he was descending to physical incarnation, mankind was experiencing the approach of the peak of the wave of philosophical materialism. "Blunt indeed became the powers of knowledge for spiritual things – most of all in the 18th century." [22] The materialistic effects of the 8th Council of Constantinople in 869-870 had by now worked through fully into western culture. The age of the archangel Gabriel, the Time Regent of the period 1510-1879, was approaching its climax. The hallmark of this period of Gabriel's influence, as always with Gabriel's Time Regencies, was to increase the degree of Man's sense of physical existence in a material world, though this time the

Christ Impulse was also able to penetrate human physical and etheric bodies through the influence of Gabriel.

During the 17th and 18th centuries the scientific and commercial revolutions took off in Britain, the most advanced European society in terms of material development. Most cultures in Europe saw a strengthening and consolidation of their physical characteristics during the same period in such areas, for example, as cuisine, dress habits, sports, and building styles. National and ethnic self-consciousness grew apace. These tendencies were accentuated during Kaspar Hauser's lifetime by the returning approach of Halley's Comet, a phenomenon which has always seemed to presage a new wave of materialism in some form. Years of the comet's return included 1066, when the Normans invaded England; 1759, at the time of the launch of the Industrial Revolution; 1835 and the railway boom, the beginnings of the chemical industry and electromagnetism; 1910 and the coming of the First World War; and 1986 and the decade of 'greed is good.' When Kaspar Hauser died in 1833, the discovery of the planet Neptune was only 13 years away and the 'War in Heaven' was set to begin in 1841. **These two events heralded a mighty effort by the ahrimanic forces in the cosmos to prepare the earth for the approaching incarnation of their master Ahriman, as mankind's 21st century neared.** Michael, archangel of the Sun, was also readying himself for his own Time Regency to take over from that of Gabriel in 1879 and to this end sought to eject the ahrimanic spirits, the angels who promoted human differentiation (nationalism, racialism) from the spiritual sphere of the Moon and cast them out and down into the earthly sphere, into the human thought world. The cosmic school of Michael, which had begun in the 15th century to prepare human souls for incarnation on Earth during the coming Age of Michael, came to an end in the late 18th century, culminating in what Rudolf Steiner called the 'Cosmic Cultus,' which was actually a super-sensible celebration of the Michaelic impulse of Anthroposophy in its descent to earth. The earthly fruits of this showed themselves already in the lives and work of the many great individualities that were active in cultural life 1750-1850. To recall the indications of Rudolf Steiner quoted above:

South Germany should have become the new Grail Castle of the new Knights of the Grail and the cradle of future events. This spiritual ground had been well-prepared by all those personalities whom we know of as Goethe, Schiller, Hölderlin, Herder and others. Kaspar Hauser was to have gathered around him, as it were, all that existed in this spiritual ground thus prepared.

The Christ Rhythm in History

'The cradle of future events' – South Germany was thus to be the seedbed of a new culture of the spiritual Ego that would grow in Europe, the heart continent of the world; Kaspar Hauser, the new Parsifal, would have been the seed and spark of that culture. Here we touch on a profound principle of the spiritual history of man. Building on Rudolf Steiner's indications in connection with the new Christian rhythm of 33 years that has been working through human history since the birth of the Nathan Jesus child, the rhythm according to which all social events are resurrected in a metamorphosed form 33 years later and then again after yet another 33 years, Pietro Archiati observed that a century (3 x 33 years) in the new 'christened' history of mankind since the birth of Jesus (humanity as the christened church) could be compared to a year in the life of an individual human being. This would mean, for example, that the 4th century would correspond to the child aged 3, the 9th century to the 8-year-old; the 1300s would correspond to the child in his 14th year, the 19th century to the 18-year-old, and the 21st century would mean that mankind at age 20 was in its 21st year of christened life, ready to receive its global Ego. There is not space here to show in detail how Archiati's observation is well borne out by historical fact, however this would not be difficult. The reader is encouraged to consider the historical events that occured in the centuries mentioned, and compare them to the corresponding ages in the developmental process of the child's biography, as discussed in anthroposophical literature on the subject of the growing child.

The three centuries from the 19th to the 21st then would represent mankind aged 18, 19, and 20. In the life of the individual the first Moon

Node occurs at 18 years and just over 6 months; this would correspond to the late 1850s, close to Rudolf Steiner's birth date of 1861. When we recall that Rudolf Steiner alluded to the fact that his original mission had not actually been the teaching of Anthroposophy as such, but rather the new Christian teaching of karma and reincarnation, we can see how he sought to help mankind to understand its origins and destiny. Just as the period of the Moon Node in an individual's biography briefly opens a window of opportunity during which the individual can glimpse something of his or her pre-natal intentions, which he inscribed into his skein of destiny in the Moon sphere before descending to earthly life, so Rudolf Steiner's biography, we can say, was just such a window of opportunity for mankind as a whole – an opportunity for self-knowledge. In 1861 Kaspar Hauser would have turned 49 and entered his Jupiter period (49-56). When Rudolf Steiner was experiencing his own Moon Node, just as the Michael Age was beginning in 1879, Kaspar Hauser would have been 67, and four years earlier in 1875 (the year the Theosophical Society was founded) would have attained the age (63) at which initiates are allowed to speak about the mysteries of karma and reincarnation. If Kaspar Hauser had lived on to the ripe old age of 92, he would perhaps have seen Rudolf Steiner take up his public work as an esoteric master. The German Prince of the Spirit could have handed on the baton, as it were, to the Central European Master of Esoteric Wisdom.

Crossing the Threshold of the Physical World: 1780-1781

Other momentous events of a far more ambiguous nature, however, which were to affect these developments profoundly, had already occurred before Kaspar Hauser's birth. According to Rudolf Steiner, human beings had formerly possessed natural clairvoyance as their birthright, but after about 3100 BC the doors of clairvoyant perception began to close. Since that time, mankind has had to find its way to the spirit in freedom, but in ever deepening spiritual darkness, except for a very few people who retained natural clairvoyance through their genetic inheritance. This period of spiritual darkness – Kali Yuga as the ancient

Hindus called it – lasted exactly 5000 years, until 1899, when the doors of natural clairvoyant perception began to open again. During the first 3100 of these 5000 years, mystery centres were established to help maintain the connection between human beings and the spiritual world through processes of initiation. With the coming of Christ to the physical plane in Jesus and His Resurrection, the mystery centres have faded away, as we have increasingly been able to find our true freedom as individuals in Christ through the passage from darkness to light.

Since 1899/1900 – the year when the 5000-year period of Kali Yuga came to an end and natural clairvoyance began to reoccur spontaneously without any kind of occult training – mankind has been steadily experiencing in this earthly life something of what it is like to be in the spiritual world after death, namely, the division of the human entelechy into its three constituent parts: thinking, feeling, and willing, as well as the sensing of non-material powers and forces. This has sometimes led to disorienting and disturbing experiences for those who go through this without prior preparation by a spiritual teaching that is in harmony with mankind's current stage of development.

* * *

About 120 years before this spiritual event of the crossing of the threshold of the *spiritual* world, and some 70-80 years before what was described above as mankind's Moon Node experience in the late 1850s, another mighty threshold was crossed in preparation for the spiritual event of 1900. This was the crossing of the *physical* threshold of the natural world in two directions – the astronomical and the sub-natural. The Industrial Revolution was based on bringing up to the surface of the Earth and into the biosphere the subterranean deposits and detritus of the Atlantean and Lemurian eras (first coal, then later gas and oil); this was already well underway in Britain when, in 1780, 33 years after Benjamin Franklin had begun his work on static electricity (1747), Galvani carried out his famous experiments with frogs' legs, which led to the discovery of electric current and were soon followed up by the primitive electric batteries of Volta. Galvani's discoveries were described by Rudolf Steiner as "the beginning of all the discoveries that rule the Earth today by means of the electric current," [23] which of course includes computers. This discovery came about through a process of which, according to Steiner, modern humanity is completely unaware – *the fact that time moves in lemniscates.* Electricity entered the human organism in the Lemurian period at the crossing point of the leminiscate of time more than 25,000 years ago, and by the late 18th century we had passed through that same point before, during the Atlantean epoch, and were now, in the 5th Post-Atlantean epoch (1413-3573), passing through it again, which was why mankind 'remembered' electricity in the discoveries of Franklin, Galvani and Volta. Electricity is a spiritual force; it is light that has 'fallen to earth' and become 'decadent.' During the First Scientific Lecture Course (23rd December 1919 - 3rd January 1920) Rudolf Steiner said that in electricity we are concerned with

> *crossing the same boundary as to the outer world as we are crossing in ourselves when we descend from our thinking and idea-forming conscious life into our life of will. All that is light, sound, and warmth is akin to our conscious life, while all that goes on in the realms of electricity and magnetism is akin – intimately akin – to our life of will.*

Mankind has been riding this wild horse of electric will ever more furiously since the 1780s, believing that it knows how to understand and master it while in fact being mastered and driven by it, for more than anything, it is electricity that has been driving the constantly accelerating and actually *inhuman* pace of modern culture. This challenge of the power of fallen light from the realm of sub nature has been one aspect of the dialectic within which our modern freedom is being tested.

The other has been the pull from the cosmic periphery. One year after Galvani's electrical experiments, in 1781, came the astonishing discovery by William Herschel of the planet Uranus, the first trans-Saturnian planet, the first planet not traditionally associated with the human soul. The ancient Egyptians and Greeks had had an inkling of the existence of Uranus in their cosmogonies, but had not actually been able to observe it physically. It was discovered in the constellation of Gemini five years after the Declaration of Independence of the new and modern nation of the United States of America. The very name 'United States' was an abstraction and this new modern state was founded on an ideology, on the basis of idealism of an abstract universal kind; it spoke of God, but of 'Nature's God,' the God of the abstract philosophy of Freemasonic Deism. The United States has since its founding been associated both with the astrological sign of Gemini and also with electricity. Interestingly, Benjamin Franklin, also famous for his electrical researches, died in 1790 at the age of 84, one orbit of Uranus. 84 is 12 x 7; in esotericism 12 is widely held to be the number of space and 7 that of time. Since space and time began together at the beginning of the Old Saturn stage of the evolution of the solar system, we can conclude that Uranus and the other two new planets do indeed in a sense stand 'outside' that evolution, despite having a relation to it. It was an American space probe, Voyager 2, that first visited Uranus in 1984. Indeed, Rudolf Steiner, in lectures given in November 1917,[24] spoke of the constellation of Gemini as the cosmic home of electromagnetism. He described then how the lodges of the western brotherhoods – the same occult lodges that sought to frustrate the mission of Kaspar Hauser – work with the forces coming from the constellation of Gemini; these are the forces that underlie cosmic dualism and all binaries, including the electrical. These forces represent a challenge and a threat to human freedom.

Uranus and electricity have a higher and lower octave. In his book *Theosophy,* describing the seven regions of Spiritland proper, Rudolf Steiner implies that the Mars Sphere is the first region of Spiritland, the Jupiter sphere the second and the Saturn sphere the third. He makes this explicit in a lecture given in Berlin on 1st April 1913.[25] Then, speaking of the fourth region of Spiritland, he says:

> *The archetypes of the fourth region are... in certain respects beings who govern the archetypes of the three lower regions and mediate their working together.*

Going on to the fifth, sixth and seventh regions, he says that:

These regions differ essentially from the preceding ones, because the beings to be found in them supply the archetypes of the lower regions with the impulses to their activity. In them we find the creative forces of the archetypes themselves... What was described in [the book] Theosophy as the fourth region of Spiritland already extends beyond our planetary system. There the soul expands into still wider spaces, into the starry firmament... There is something so utterly foreign in what is conveyed by the fourth region of Spiritland that it can never correspond with what can be experienced even within the outermost planetary sphere, the Saturn sphere.

At first sight, since he says that "the fourth region of Spiritland already extends beyond our planetary system," this would seem to suggest that the fourth region could not be the sphere of Uranus, as Uranus also orbits the Sun. And yet for Steiner, Saturn not Neptune (Pluto had not yet been discovered in 1913) was "the outermost planetary sphere." Uranus, Neptune and Pluto do in fact exhibit very anomalous astronomical characteristics, which make one question whether they belong to the solar system in the same sense as the traditional celestial bodies.

The astrosopher Willi Sucher tentatively related the trans-Saturnian planets to the three higher spiritual faculties of Man: Uranus – Imagination and Spirit Self; Neptune – Inspiration and Life Spirit; Pluto – Intuition and Spirit Man. These three planetary spheres, he wrote, mediated to Man purely spiritual impulses from the higher realms of the Zodiac. If these impulses are not received by the human being consciously, they can easily wreak 'destruction' and thereby bring home all too forcefully the temporariness of Earth-material existence. Certainly, Sucher's insight might appear borne out if one contemplates the historical phenomena that occurred at the time these three planets were discovered. To name but a few of the main events:

Uranus: The relatively sudden emergence of the USA in the American Revolution (the decisive battle, at Yorktown, was fought and won in 1781)

The discovery of electricity (1781)

The events of the French Revolution suggestive of sudden and drastic change (1789-1794)

The last auto-da-fé of the Spanish Inquisition (1781)

The comet-like rise and fall of Napoleon (1794-1815)

Neptune: The Opium Wars (1839-1842, 1858-1860)

The beginnings of Marxism and Spiritualism (1848)

The development of the chemical industry and of electro-magnetism (1840's)

The development and spread of railways (1840's)

Pluto: The Great Crash (1929)

Hitler and Stalin (1930's)

The splitting of the atom and the development of atomic energy (1930's).

These developments enable a more significant imagination to come into view, namely, that *the appearance to mankind of these three planets has something in common with the appearance of the three Magi in the New Testament.* As those three *human* beings appeared before the One who was to bear the Christ, Lord of the Worlds, so three mighty spiritual beings (or communities of beings) appeared before mankind as it approached its Moon Node in the mid-19th century and approaches its '21st birthday' in the year 2100. This latter event signifies 'the birth,' or appearance, of the Ego of humanity, for from the 1930s of the 20th century onwards, human perception of the Etheric Christ, at first limited to very few people, will steadily grow as the doors of natural clairvoyant perception mentioned above, open ever wider. This is the Second Coming of Christ, an event that will develop over many centuries, this time not in the physical, but in the etheric realm of the Earth – the invisible biosphere; in the New Testament, it is referred to as the coming 'in the clouds.' We shall later see how this event relates to the deed of Kaspar Hauser.

Like the human Magi, the three new planets too brought gifts, but gifts which were ambiguous and two-sided, and which depended for their use on Man's state of consciousness. For the three higher faculties of Imagination, Inspiration and Intuition, which can be related to Uranus, Neptune and Pluto respectively, are also mirrored in their opposites: the threefold powers of luciferic *temptation*, ahrimanic *enslavement*, and asuric *annihilation* organised in the nine divisions of the three subterranean realms of the Earth. As above, so below: above, beyond Saturn – the source of the three spiritual gifts of Imagination, Inspiration and Intuition; and below, in the interior of the Earth, their fallen correlates – the sources of temptation, enslavement and annihilation. Between them is the threefold soul of Man in thinking, feeling and willing, striving for freedom. We can therefore suppose that the fourth region of Spiritland is that of the sphere of Uranus, the fifth that of Neptune, and the sixth that of Pluto; the seventh region takes us beyond into the realm of the Zodiac proper.

* * *

The epochal year 1781 also saw the first performance of Schiller's first play *The Robbers*:

> *"The theatre was like a madhouse – rolling eyes, clenched fists, and hoarse cries in the auditorium," wrote an eye-witness. "Strangers fell sobbing into each other's arms, women on the point of fainting staggered towards the exit. There was a universal commotion as in chaos, out of the mists of which a new creation bursts forth." The English Romantics, especially Coleridge, greatly admired the play and saluted its theme of liberty. Coleridge wrote: "Who is this Schiller? This Convulser of the Heart?"* [26]

Twenty-four years later Schiller was dead – killed, according to Rudolf Steiner, by the 'dark forces' of 'Illuminist Jesuits,' during the writing of his play *Demetrius*, the theme of which was the mystery of the young idealist Dmitri, the Russian would-be Czar who seized power in

1604-1605 [27] – it was the story of a problem of identity as mysterious as that of Kaspar Hauser.

The Massacre of the Innocents

Just as the three gifts of the human Magi were accompanied by the inhuman deed of Herod in the massacre of the innocents, the approach of the cosmic Magi was accompanied by the inhuman intensification of the enslavement and wilful destruction of human beings (on the American continent, the slavery of the Negroes and the destruction of the native Indian tribes; in Europe, children worked to death in factories and mines, especially in Britain; and in Asia, the lives of Chinese opium addicts ruined or destroyed in their millions). Was this not another massacre of the innocents? Were not all these appalling deeds going on throughout the life of Kaspar Hauser? The very year of his death saw the beginnings of the colossal effort to roll them back. In 1833, after a struggle lasting decades, slavery was finally abolished throughout the British Empire, and loopholes were closed in the Factory Acts in Britain; it became illegal to employ children under nine years old, and children between nine and thirteen were barred from working more than nine hours a day(!). Those between twelve and eighteen were now 'only' allowed to work twelve hours a day. By 1866, 33 years after the death of Kaspar Hauser, the American Civil War was won and slavery ended in the USA, though the massacre of the Indians went on. In 1833 the British government took over responsibility for the opium trade from the East India Company; this led directly within seven years to the First Opium War. The legal opium trade between Britain and China was not ended until 1917 – the year that Rudolf Steiner specifically related to 1841, when the War in Heaven began and the Opium War was raging on Earth.[28] The catastrophic events of 1917, he said, referring particularly to the Russian revolutions, were the direct karmic result of the triumph of materialism in the early 1840s. By 1917, millions of Chinese had died as a direct or indirect result of the opium trade. The karma of opium then can also be traced back to the years of Kaspar Hauser's lifetime and the karma of western materialism as Britain's addiction to tea drinking and its profit led it to enslave China in opium. Within 100 years of Kaspar Hauser's death, all three of these blots on humanity, these massacres of the innocents (American slavery and genocide, European child labour, the legal opium trade in Asia) had been stopped, but Stalin and Hitler had only just begun...

Mars and Mercury

Another cosmic aspect of the time in which Kaspar Hauser lived is the fact that, according to Rudolf Steiner, during the last of the seven epochs of Lemuria – thus during the age of cosmic time when electricity was implanted in the human astral body as a result of the Fall – the etheric streams of the planet Mars passed through the Earth sphere; this was the cosmic origin of the iron in the body of the Earth. After the departure of the moon from the Earth during Lemuria, the planet Mars passed through the Earth, and so to say, left iron behind. We can think that etheric streams radiated from Mars to Earth and, interacting with the form principle of iron governed by the Spirits of Form, gave rise to earthly iron.

This laying down of iron into the Earth provided part of the basis of human blood, and thus for the human ego which indwells the blood. Mars, the spiritual power that initiates and impels new budding develop-ments, is therefore connected to the human ability to follow the Rosicrucian path. This mystery of Mars has to do with the sacrifice of the Gautama Buddha being in the year 1604 on the planet Mars, where, Rudolf Steiner relates, the Buddha was sent to pacify the turbulence that had developed there, which was increasingly tending to divide the human souls descending through the heavenly spheres to earthly incarnation.[29] During the mediaeval period, human souls were becoming increasingly polarised into two groups: those with little connection to the earth and those whose connection was too strong. In Western society the Franciscans and the Jesuits respectively were examples of these tendencies. In mediaeval Japanese Buddhism, the devotional Pure Land Schools and the militant Nichiren sect can be seen as representing a similar polarity. If these tendencies had continued, the Rosicrucian stream would never have

been able to implant itself firmly in human souls. This is why the Buddha's sacrificial activity on Mars, which Steiner described as being tantamount to a crucifixion experience for him, began in the year 1604, the year when in Europe, the Rosicrucian movement can be said to have begun.

The cosmic harbinger of these great events seemed to be the sighting of the supernova in the constellation Ophiuchus observed by Kepler on 17th October that year and subsequently known as Kepler's Star. He studied it extensively and wrote a book about it called *De Stella nova in pede Serpentarii* (*On the new star in the Serpent's foot*). Rudolf Steiner described in some detail how the Buddha had helped to prepare mankind for the coming of the Christ and how the Events of Palestine signified a colossal shift in the evolution of the Earth from the influence of Mars, during the incarnating phase of Earth's development, to Mercury, during the excarnating phase. Indeed, 'Mars-Mercury,' he says, is the esoteric name for the Earth. Both the Buddha and the Christ had appeared during the Age of Aries (747 BC – 1413 AD), the Buddha near the beginning of that age and the Christ a third of the way through it. It is thus the basis of Earth evolution itself that the necessarily divisive and individuating impulse of Mars is followed by the healing, mediating and reconciling principle of Mercury, quicksilver, the metal which Georg Friedrich Daumer noted was particularly loved by his pupil, Kaspar Hauser. Rudolf Steiner described Daumer as 'the last Rosicrucian.' [30]

Napoleon

We have seen that a kind of recurrence of a period of Lemurian development was happening during the late 18th century. A similar 'collision' with a powerful Mars force can be seen in the stormy passage of Napoleon across the stage of world history. He was born in 1769 and died at the age of 51 in 1821, thus having completed his Mars phase (42-49) but not his Jupiter phase (49-56). The Mars force is that which divides, separates, individuates and condenses. Napoleon was born on the island of Corsica in the middle of the Mediterranean and, though he sought to become emperor of a continent, he eventually died in exile on another island – the isolated St Helena in the middle of the Atlantic. A military genius of seemingly unstoppable brilliance and dynamism, he was yet an enigmatic figure. Rudolf Steiner was unable to trace his previous incarnations and said that he was a powerful Mars spirit (that is, one who had had powerful experiences in the Mars sphere between death and a new birth) who had 'forgotten his mission.' In 1604 the Buddha had brought Mercury forces to Mars. One hundred and sixty-five years, that is, one orbit of Neptune later, Napoleon brought only Mars to Mercury-Earth. Napoleon forgot his mission; it was desired by sinister forces that Kaspar Hauser should be made to forget his.

The relationship between Mars and Mercury can also be seen in the intertwined destinies of Napoleon and Kaspar Hauser. It was Napoleon who brought Kaspar's parents together in a political marriage to suit his dynastic aims. He arranged the union of Stephanie de Beauharnais, his adopted daughter and Karl of Baden, heir to the throne of Baden. It was also Napoleon who took the Palatinate from Bavaria in 1803 and gave it to Baden, thus sowing the seeds of resentment in Crown prince Ludwig of Bavaria that would play such an important role in Kaspar's destiny; the Palatinate had been Ludwig's childhood home for 10 years, from 3 until 13. Finally, Napoleion's own son, Napoleon II, 'the King of Rome' and Duke of Reichstadt, was fated to share Kaspar's fate in a sense, except that the 'cage' he was kept in at Schönbrunn Palace in Vienna was gilded. Here he was to remain, separated from his mother like Kaspar, and under the watchful eye of the Austrian Chancellor, Metternich, until his own death at 21 – the same age as Kaspar. In 1789, the year the Revolution broke out, Napoleon turned 21. The period 1794-1815, which saw his rise to absolute power, lasted 21 years. Kaspar, who died at 21, was born in 1812, while Napoleon died in 1821.

Kaspar was born when Napoleon, at age 43, had just entered the Mars phase of his own biography. When Napoleon died in 1821, Kaspar, at age 9, was in the Mercury period of his life, a period which he was forced to live through in darkness and silence. Thirty-three years after the death of Napoleon, the western Powers, Britain and France, the latter led by Emperor Napoleon III, launched their assault on Russia in the Crimean

War (1854-1856) – the very same aggression that Napoleon had been engaged in when Kaspar was born (in 1860 the same two Powers would jointly make war on China). Thirty-three years after the death of Kaspar Hauser, Bismarck's Prussia crushed Austria in the Austro-Prussian War of 1866; this was the result, as has been discussed above, of Kaspar Hauser's mercurial influence not being present as it should have been. Prussia's victory over Austria seemed to have settled once and for all the issue of the form of Central Europe – should there be a greater Germany (including Austria) or a small Germany (without Austria and focused on Prussia)? This had been a matter of debate since Napoleon, 60 years before in 1806, had abolished the 1000-year-old Holy Roman Empire founded by Charlemagne. The dualistic polity of Austria-Hungary, 'the impossible state' created by the *Ausgleich* (Compromise) of 1867, and founded on the joint domination by two ethnic groups of many other smaller ones, was the direct result of Austria being 'ejected' by Prussia from the rest of the German-speaking area. This was to lead eventually to the tinderbox Balkan politics that provided the spark for the Great War, 3 x 33 years after the defeat of Napoleon. The Mars spirit of Napoleon was destined to play its part in European history before the Mercury spirit of Kaspar Hauser could bring its healing impulse to bear. This too was surely known by those forces ranged against Kaspar Hauser's mission. But Kaspar's mission in southern Germany

> ... was not wanted by those circles (the western lodges and the Jesuits). They could not tolerate a centre that was awakening to consciousness if they were not to relinquish their power and designs for power. A spirit such as Goethe's frightened them. <u>Napoleon forced them to unite</u> [emphasis – TMB] and form a league for the aspired-to world domination in the spheres of commerce and ideology. Napoleon had already thwarted their effort; it was he who fundamentally forces the two currents into union. From that time onwards the tasks allotted to each were clearly circumscribed. But for that their clearly defined goal of world domination became all the more effective. The ideological and spiritual affairs were given into the hands of the Jesuits; the commercial ones into the hands of the Anglo-American

Lodges of the West. These plans, however, will lead to ever more tragic catastrophes, because none of them take human development into account. What was intended to happen through Kaspar Hauser was overthrown by mankind.[31]

The NAROS cycle

A third cosmic event of which the occultists among the opponents of Kaspar Hauser's mission must have been aware was the *Naros* (or *Neros*) cycle. Historically, the Naros cycle represents a lunisolar cycle of 31 periods of 19 years and one period of 11 years, making 600 years of either 7200 solar months, 7421 lunar months or 219,145/6 solar days. The 600 year cycle represents a renewal of the conjunction of the sun and planets on a new moon at the vernal equinox. The ancient Chaldeans were credited with the discovery of this grand epoch, which can be broken down into ten periods of sixty years each, or, alternately, into a dozen periods of fifty years each. Various cultures have consequently relied upon the Naros cycle to delineate the transition of one historical age into another.

One of the most knowledgeable western scholars of esoterica during the lifetime of Kaspar Hauser was Godfrey Higgins (1772-1833). Higgins was an army officer, an MP, traveller, writer, philanthropist and an active Freemason who was close to the Duke of Sussex (1773-1843), widely regarded as the leading Freemason of the age. The Duke, sixth son of King George III, President of the Royal Society, and Grand Master of United Grand Lodge for several decades until his death in 1843, dominated the British Freemasonry of his day. Higgins said of him that "there were but two Masons in England – himself and the Duke of Sussex."[32] The Duke had extensive contacts on the Continent, notably with the Jewish Lodge at Frankfurt to which he granted a new unrestricted charter in 1817. Like Higgins, he strove throughout his Masonic career to divest Freemasonry of all remaining Christian elements and was opposed to those Continental and notably Germanic Masonic streams – such as the new 'Templar' and 'Rosicrucian' Orders – that insisted on Christianised rituals. The Duke was an ostensible supporter of most of the progressive causes of the day, a keen scholar of the Kabbalah, a good friend of the leading Jewish families, notably the Rothschilds, and a champion of Jewish emancipation in Britain. It was also the Duke who in 1813 reunited under his leadership the two branches of British Freemasonry, which had been in dispute since the 1750s. This man, who has perhaps the best title to the position of leading occultist in Britain during the life of Kaspar Hauser, was close to such figures as Nathan Rothschild, Adam Czartoryski, and Europe's leading propagandist, the Prussian Friedrich von Gentz (of whom, more later). Higgins said of the Duke of Sussex:

> *Why do the priest-led monarchs of the continent persecute Masonry? Is it because they are not entrusted with its secrets; or, because their priests cannot make it subservient to their base purposes? All these questions I may ask, gentle reader; but all I may not answer. If you be not satisfied, ask his Royal Highness the Duke of Sussex; he can answer IF HE CHOOSES [emphasis by Higgins – TMB]. But this I may say, it is not every apprentice or fellow-craft who knows all the secrets of Masonry.* [33]

Higgins and the Duke shared the view that all religions were one at the source and that Christianity, with its priests, dogmas, sects and confessions had only obscured this fact. The rationalism of the two men inclined to a kind of Deist Unitarianism that could embrace all faiths and beliefs. Higgins believed that the Chaldees (Chaldeans) and the Druid Order known as the 'Culdees' were one and the same. He held the Culdees to be the original British Druidic Masons and 'discovered' that the last lodge meeting of this venerable body had been held in his own lifetime, on 27th May 1778. He entrusted to the Duke a number of important documents relating to these Masonic origins. Needless to say, the two men also believed that Britain was the land that preserved this true original and universal religion of Man and that the 'organic' British Constitution upheld and guaranteed it. It is not difficult, therefore, to see why the Duke should have considered that if Britain's empire was to be truly universal, its Masonic faith should also be, and so he therefore strove mightily to expunge all references to Christianity from Freemasonry in order to turn it into what might be called a One World Philosophy or Religion to which all men of quality could feel called.

The beginning of each Naros cycle was held to portend the birth of *a great avatar,* or spiritual leader, for that culture. In his major work *Anacalypsis* (1833) Higgins describes the Jewish cycle of Naros beginning with Enoch. The second Naros cycle ended with the birth of Noah and the third with Noah leaving the Ark when he was 600 years old. The fourth ended about the time of Melchizedek, that high priest of God whom Higgins placed at the end of the seventh cycle with Elijah, like Melchizedek, another immortal prophet. The eighth cycle began about 600 B.C. with the birth of Cyrus, the Persian king who liberated the Jews from the Babylonian Captivity. The ninth cycle began with the birth of Jesus. This made eight complete cycles of 600 years each before the birth of the Messiah. Higgins does not mention the tenth avatar, but Mohammed is held to have been born in 570 AD. Certainly, the period around 600 BC was a remarkable time that witnessed the activity of many great spirits. In India, there was Gautama Buddha; in China, Confucius, and in Greece, Heraclitus and Pythagoras. This parallel development of the Jewish, Greek, and Buddhist streams was overseen by the archangel Michael who had until that time been the Folk Spirit of the People of Israel before becoming the Time Regent – of the period c. 600 – c. 200 BC.

The following Naros cycles were thus due in approximately the year 1200, when across the world another great cadre of adepts appeared in various countries (e.g. the Franciscans and Dominicans in Europe and the Zen and Nichiren Buddhist Schools in Japan) and again in 1800. It was this 19th century occurrence that contemporary occultic writers such as Higgins were aware of. Michael as Time Regent had from 600 BC prepared the way for the Christ. Around 1800 another Naros cycle began with yet another tremendous down pouring of great spirits that paved the way for Michael's resumption of his Time Lordship in 1879. Each Time Regency lasts for some 350-400 years. Four hundred years from 1879 is 2279 and 600 years from 1800 is 2400. This Naros cycle and the age of Michael thus roughly coincide. The question we can consider is: *Was Kaspar Hauser the avatar of this new Naros cycle,* the Adept among the great spirits who were active in Europe in the first third of the 19th century, whose coming was awaited by all those with occult knowledge? Was his incarnation foreseen, and were plans laid in advance to forestall it and frustrate his mission?

Chapter 5

Enemies and Allies

Kaspar Hauser's Enemies: Groups

Before looking at some of the remarkable constellation of individualities that prepared the spiritual-cultural space of Central Europe prior to the birth of Kaspar Hauser, and in the light of what has been presented above about the Naros cycle, let us consider who might well have been among those who, more or less consciously, sought to prevent his mission.

Ludwig Polzer-Hoditz made the following notes of a conversation he had had with Rudolf Steiner in November 1916: "Those circles which conceal everything and today still try to conceal what happened with Kaspar Hauser's destiny, are those members of western lodges and Jesuits who have worked together in their leading organisations for more than 150 years, but demonstrably since January 1802." [34] "...more than 150 years..." implies that the two groups have been working together since at least 1766. That takes us back to the last time when Christian Rosenkreutz (in his incarnation as Count St Germain) was recorded by external history as having been at work in cultural and political events. At the beginning of the 1760's he was seeking (in alliance with those around Louis XV, but opposed by the King's Minister, the Duc de Choiseul) to bring an end to the Seven Years' War, referred to by some historians as the real First World War, as Britain and France battled each other on three continents. It also takes us to the era when the fortunes of Freemasonry in Britain and the Society of Jesus suffered severe setbacks. A major split opened up within

British Freemasonry in the 1750s between the 'Moderns' and the so-called 'Antients,' which was not healed until 1816, when the Duke of Sussex achieved it and became Grand Master of a reunited Grand Lodge, a post he held until his death in 1843. Meanwhile, the Society of Jesus, which, since its formation in 1540 had been the right hand and most obedient servant of the Papacy, was actually dissolved by Pope Clement XIV in 1773 as a result of Masonic infiltration of the ruling elites of the Catholic powers of France, Spain, and Portugal.

During their period in the wilderness, the Jesuits surprisingly found succour at the Lutheran and Russian Orthodox courts of 'the two Greats' – Frederick the Great of Prussia and Catherine the Great of Russia. By these two monarchs, who were then making strenuous efforts to increase their countries' power and status, the Jesuits' educational skills were especially prized, and they managed to hold out until, along with the Inquisition, they were reinstated by Pope Pius VII in 1814. Interestingly, in the one period for which there is documentary evidence of the activity of Count St Germain in the public arena – the mid to late 18th century – the two groups that were overshadowed by the luciferic and ahrimanic powers both suffered severe difficulties. Soon after the birth of Kaspar Hauser, however, they both overcame these difficulties and returned to their former positions of concentrated influence; indeed, the nineteenth century proved, arguably, to be their period of greatest influence.

The agreement between these fiercely antagonistic occult groups which, according to Steiner, showed demonstrably from January 1802 that elements within them were working together was one by which the two groups resolved on a certain 'cooperation,' in that control of spiritual and cultural affairs was to be given over to the Jesuits while the determination of economic affairs was to be steered by the western Freemasonic brotherhoods.

Those who desire to work in this way are always concerned, not to stimulate just one stream but to make sure that one stream is always crossed by another, so that they influence each other in some way. Not much is achieved by simply running straight ahead with a single stream. It is necessary sometimes to throw a sidelight on this stream so that certain things become confused, so that certain tracks are covered up, and other things are lost in an impenetrable thicket. This is very important. Thus it comes about that certain secret streams which have set themselves some task or other also set about achieving the exact opposite. These opposing streams have the effect of obliterating all tracks. I could point to a place in Europe where so-called Freemasonry, so-called secret societies, had a great influence at a certain time when significant things were going on; certain people were acting under the suggestive influence of certain Masonic societies with an occult background. It was then necessary to obliterate the tracks at this point. So a certain Jesuit influence was brought to play so that Masonic and Jesuit influences met; for there are higher instances, 'empires,' which can quite well make use of both Masons and Jesuits in order to achieve what they want to achieve through the collaboration of the two. Do not believe that there can be no individuals who are both Jesuit and Freemason. They have progressed beyond the point of working in one direction only. They know that it is necessary to tackle situations from various sides in order to push matters in a particular direction.[35]

It is significant for the present discussion that Rudolf Steiner made these remarks in the context of speaking about Peter the Great and the so-called Testament of Peter the Great, a forged document emanating from France – via a Polish connection – that purported to show the basis of a Russian plan for world domination; this plan was used by Napoleon to justify his invasion of Russia in 1812. It is unlikely that Napoleon knew of the real origin of the document; historians have not yet ascertained whether he did.[36] What was left of Catholic Poland in 1793 (the country had already lost territory to the monarchies of Austria, Prussia and Russia in the First Partition of Poland 1772) was allied to the revolutionary and later imperial power of France (countless Poles fought willingly for Napoleon against their perceived oppressors, the Russians, Prussians and Austrians), while Freemasonry of an increasingly atheistic nature had made great inroads into French society since the days of Voltaire and *les philosophes;* one has only to recall Robespierre and his cult of Reason and

the Supreme Being, a cult that owed very much to the Deism of English Masonry and the Masonic veneration for Isis and other female divinities such as Demeter or Ceres. The point here is that as 'the Child of Europe' was about to be born, the occult forces of Masonry and Jesuitism were cooperating to bring about an assault by the West against the East, in which the peoples of Central Europe were to be forced to collaborate.

It is instructive that Rudolf Steiner referred to the Testament of Peter the Great <u>after</u> June 1916. June that year saw the death of General Helmuth von Moltke, former Chief of the German General Staff until his dismissal by the Kaiser in November 1914 after the loss of the Battle of the Marne. Von Moltke's wife Eliza was an esoteric pupil of Rudolf Steiner's, and her husband had entered anthroposophical circles through her. Rudolf Steiner read a special prayer at his funeral and thereafter was in spiritual contact with von Moltke's soul. The nature and content of their communications was published by Thomas Meyer in his book *Light for the New Millennium – Rudolf Steiner's Association with Helmuth and Eliza von Moltke.*[37]

We are here put in mind of Rudolf Steiner's remarks about the supreme importance for the future of world development of the relationship between Central and Eastern Europe, especially Russia, in the coming 6th Post-Atlantean epoch (3573-5733) and attempts by occult forces in the west to frustrate this development by preventing the growth of a healthy relationship between these two cultures. The West, or rather those elite forces that would dominate and lead it, have thus sought to create direct links between western and eastern Europe that cut out central Europe. Peter the Great, who studied in England and Holland, was under esoteric influence from his western advisors, (notably Scotsmen Jacob Bruce (1669-1735), described by Pushkin as a 'Russian faust' and Robert Erskine (1677-1718)). Peter's westernisation of Russia was facilitated by such advisors. Napoleon and most of his male relatives are known to have been Freemasons, and the Napoleonic invasion of Russia was another attempt to inject western 'Enlightenment' values into Russia while bypassing Central Europe. Karl Marx may have been a *German* Jew, but his political philosophy and economic analysis, his great work *Capital* and his three main principles of class war, historical materialism, and surplus value are unthinkable without their being anchored by Marx in the experience and phenomena of Victorian England. These communist ideas were seeded in Russia from Western Europe; they do not owe anything of significance to the cultural heritage of Central Europe. The Masonic configuration of the Provisional government that took power in Russia in February 1917 is well-known to academics, as is the role of the British and U.S. authorities in facilitating the return of Trotsky to Russia and in undermining the white anti-Bolshevik father in the Russian Civil War, followed by American economic support for the Bolshevik regime in the 1920's.[38]

The significance of Helmuth von Moltke and his death in June 1916 is that Rudolf Steiner knew that von Moltke had in his previous incarnation been Pope Nicholas I (858-867), who had been responsible for *separating* Central and Eastern Europe in the 9th century in order that Central Europe should be able to develop its own culture without being unduly influenced by the Eastern Orthodox spirit of Byzantium. If the spirit of Byzantium, represented in Nicholas' time by the great Orthodox monks Cyril and Methodius, had been able to spread unchecked throughout Central Europe, then Europe as a whole would eventually have developed a twofold not a threefold spiritual culture. Helmuth von Moltke had not only been sent as a young man by the Kaiser on an alliance-seeking mission to Russia; as Chief of the German General Staff in August 1914, he was responsible for overseeing the *attack* of the German army against the West this time, and the *defence* against the Russian attack in the East. Where he had succeeded in his aims in the 9th century, he failed in the 20th; the German attack in the West broke down, leading to a four-year stalemate on the Western Front and, ultimately, to the utter defeat of Central Europe and the end of the German and Austro-Hungarian Empires. The western occult forces directing Britain, France and the USA, however, largely achieved their goals: victory over both Central Europe and Eastern Europe, as Bolshevism was successfully transplanted into Russia and their great long-planned socialist experiment, which would last 72 years, began to unfold.[39]

This effort by the occult forces of the West to override Central

Europe is the principle of the cooperation of black (the physical) and white (the spiritual) in which the mediating red (the human middle, the heart's blood) is left out. It is noteworthy that these three **colours** would later, from 1871, become those of the German Empire, although in the order, from top to bottom, of black, white, red. Decadent spiritual forces and economic forces were to cooperate in the Jesuit-Masonic scheme, and the human heart would be crushed between them; this is the normal mode of working of the counter-forces: a luciferic spirit and an ahrimanic materialism combine to confuse, delude and enslave the human soul: there is always the effort to squeeze out and destroy the mediating middle element, whatever form that that middle element may take. The British researcher Prof. Anthony C. Sutton (formerly of Stanford University) usefully drew attention to the ways in which, in the 20th century, the American secret society Skull and Bones (founded 1832-1833, the year of Kaspar Hauser's death, and the society to which both President George W. Bush and his father belong) made use of this same principle of black and white, which, unfortunately, Sutton confused with Hegel's dialectic. It is indeed a dialectic of sorts, but not one that Hegel would have espoused. He saw the dialectic as the movement of the Spirit through world history, not as an instrument of Machiavellian manipulation.[40]

Kaspar Hauser's Enemies: Individuals

It might seem as if the obvious individual enemies of Kaspar Hauser were those such as the teacher Meyer, the violent servant of the Baden Court, Major Hennenhofer, or the police officer Hickel, all of whom directly attacked him physically or psychologically. Then there are those involved in the dynastic crime against him at a higher level, who made use of the above three: Lord Stanhope who was clearly acting for the court of Baden and the Grand Duchess Sophie of Baden, who in effect employed Stanhope as an agent. She was acting for her weak-willed husband Grand Duke Leopold, who was only Grand Duke because his mother, the Countess Hochberg and her lover, Grand Duke Ludwig, had set Kaspar aside and replaced him with a substitute doomed to die so that they could take power – Ludwig directly and the Countess through her descendants. Then there was Crown Prince Ludwig of Bavaria (King Ludwig I 1825-1848) who sought to use Kaspar Hauser as a pawn in his territorial dispute with Baden over the Sponheim area of the Palatinate. But all these people, including Stanhope, important agent though he was, were actually only instruments in the hands of more powerful forces. They did not have the knowledge of why Kaspar was important, and were only following their own petty personal agendas; Stanhope, for example, an aristocrat whose own father had declined to make provision for him in his will, was always desperate for money, and the financial need to support himself and his young family without his estranged father's aid or inheritance had first taken him into intelligence work for the British government in March 1812, when he embarked at Portsmouth for a mission to Sicily. Meyer and Hickel were paid by Stanhope, who was himself paid by Baden banks but also worked for higher authorities than the court of Baden, for he was obliged both to the British Foreign Office through his family connections and also to the Habsburg court in Vienna via Friedrich Gentz and his master Prince Metternich. These two cynical and world-weary men, though not religious themselves, worked from Vienna, where the Jesuit Order had traditionally been strong, against Munich, capital of the largely Catholic Kingdom of Bavaria – long embroiled in a vicious feud with Baden over possession of the Palatinate. It is in these higher centres of London, Vienna and Munich that Kaspar Hauser's more significant enemies, the real string-pullers, are to be sought.

Lord Stanhope

The date of January 1802 given by Rudolf Steiner as the time when those forces opposed to Kaspar Hauser effectively began to collaborate[41] provides a useful point at which to begin to investigate the individuals most likely to have been involved in the effort to frustrate the mission of Kaspar Hauser. He was killed when he was 21, and 21 years before 1802, the year 1781 saw the groundbreaking work of Galvani in electricity, the discovery by Herschel of the planet Uranus (quickly associated by astrologers with the new energy of electricity due to its eccentric astronomical characteristics); it also saw the birth (7th December) of Philip Henry, 4th Earl of Stanhope. Stanhope was to die on 2nd March 1855, that is, 21 years after the death of Kaspar Hauser (17th December 1833). Peter Tradowsky described Stanhope as "the demon of the English spirit as Hitler was the counter picture of the German spirit." [42] While this may seem to overstate Stanhope's individual spiritual significance compared to the man who unleashed World War II, both Stanhope and Hitler, who became Chancellor of Germany in 1933, played their part in trying to prevent the incarnation in Central Europe of the free ego of modern humanity, which Kaspar Hauser in his time represented. It could also be said that in fact both world wars are in their origins not unrelated to Stanhope's actions: World War II cannot be separated from World War I (they have been called the 30 Years' War of the 20th Century), while World War I resulted in large part from the intention of the British elite to frustrate the rise to power of an unbalanced imperial Germany, this new Germany merely sought to emulate Britain's imperial successes because, like Napoleon, it had forgotten its own mission. There is not the space here to go into the British diplomatic revolution that prepared the scenario of July 1914; for an exoteric discussion of it, see E.E. McCullough, *How the First World War Began.*[43] Kaspar Hauser had represented the mission of Germany and he had been removed through the agency of Stanhope. The English lord did not commit the murder himself, but his skilful techniques of seduction were employed to remove Kaspar from the protection of his friends (and the police) in Nuremberg to a more isolated and unprotected situation in Ansbach, where he was eventually murdered. Like his collaborators Metternich and Gentz in Vienna, and most unlike his own very eccentric and politically very radical father, Philip Henry Stanhope was a conservative to his core. He said of himself: "I am one of those old fashioned Tories, who wish that Rights may be respected, all Property may be secured and that ancient institutions may be preserved." [44]

In Mahon's eyes, the future was always gloomy and fateful; revolution and misfortune were always to be expected. His political confession of faith: "a Tory of Mr Pitt's school" is not without significance in the story of Kaspar Hauser. Insofar as Pitt had pursued and conceived of his European policy and the struggle with Napoleon, his easily influenced admirer [Stanhope] was, in his political thinking, the exact counterpart and mouthpiece of the Lord Chancellor. The question of what political interest Stanhope could have had in the case of Kaspar Hauser is to be looked for and found in this direction.[45]

In other words, Stanhope, who could trace his descent back to the Norman Conquest and directly to King Henry III and Robert the Bruce in the 13th century, was a quintessential representative of the aristocratic oligarchical, and ultra-conservative element in British life that is determined at all costs to preserve its privileges, social standing and gilded lifestyle. In this sense, Tradowsky was perhaps right to call him 'the demon of the English spirit.' Stanhope was a tool in the hands of those forces that wished to establish the binary principle of black and white in modern life and that sought to prevent the emergence of a culture based on a healthy Trinitarian or triadic principle. The motto of Liberty, Equality, and Fraternity was a first, inchoate, stammering enunciation of the threefold Rosicrucian ideal in the modern age, and the murder of Kaspar Hauser was thus one of the most significant obstacles deliberately placed in the way of the realisation of a culture based on that threefold ideal.

The binary principle had been enunciated by the English philosopher-statesman Francis Bacon in the early 17th century. In his writings on cryptography he declared that all human thinking could be reduced to a series of A's and B's [46] – a notion that would later form the basis of the binary system of computers. This binary thinking was physically underpinned by the nature of electricity, discovered along with the planet Uranus in 1781. Interestingly, in the year of Kaspar Hauser's death 1833, Charles Babbage started work on his 'analytical engine' – the first mechanical general computer, which was never completed. He was assisted in this by the woman who he said could explain his engine better than he could himself and who is often described as the world's first computer programmer – Ada, Lady Lovelace, daughter of that most martial of poets, Lord Byron.

Friedrich von Gentz

Twenty-one years after 1781 then, came the year which Rudolf Steiner indicated as demonstrating the cooperation of Freemasons and Jesuits. In May 1802 the Prussian royal advisor Friedrich von Gentz (1764-1832) moved from Prussia to Vienna. Von Gentz was a brilliant writer and publicist; a direct pupil of Immanuel Kant, having studied for two years under the master in Königsberg, and an admirer of Edmund Burke, he was very pro-British and detested Napoleon and all his works. With close connections to many in the Masonic world but not himself apparently one of the Brethren, Gentz was described as loving "men often, women sometimes, and money always." He was a notorious bisexual lover of many in the glitterati as well as being a member of the original Tugendbund (League of Virtue), a crypto-Masonic group of 'freethinkers,' some of whose members engaged in activities that were somewhat less than what was normally considered 'virtuous behaviour.' Gentz had begun his political career in Prussia as a moderate conservative very much influenced by the ideas of Edmund Burke, whose works he translated to great effect, but with the rise of Napoleon, and particularly after his own relocation to Vienna, he moved steadily to the right. He was an astute and insightful observer of contemporary events, whose views sometimes bordered on real intuition. His farsightedness may have stemmed from his association with men with occult insight, as evidenced by his view of a future dominated by England and America. He regarded the separation of America from England as indispensable for this:

> *The eternal and virtuous empire of English commerce, founded on the free exchange of commodities and credit, had been made possible, in [Gentz's] view, by the independence of the North American colonies in 1783. He repeated, in pamphlet after pamphlet, that 'the loss of her colonies was the first aera of the lasting and independent greatness of Britain,' and 'the first complete demonstration of the true principles of the wealth of nations.' Freed of monopoly power, and of the oppression of formal empire, England and her former colonies could constitute a lasting union, of language and principles.*[47]

The reference to the 'wealth of nations' signalled to his readers that he had read, as indeed he had – and digested – long before others in Germany, Adam Smith's *Wealth of Nations* (1776).

The knowledge [Gentz] displayed of the principles and practice of finance was especially remarkable. In 1797, at the instance of English statesmen, he published a translation of a history of French finance by Francois d'Ivernois, an eminent Genevese exile naturalized and knighted in England... Opposition to France was the inspiring principle of the Historisches Journal *founded by him in 1799-1800, which once more held up English institutions as the model, and became in Germany the mouthpiece of British policy towards the revolutionary aggressions of the French republic.*[48]

He put his brilliant abilities as a propagandist increasingly in the service of ultra-conservative causes, becoming in 1812, the year of Kaspar Hauser's birth, the right-hand man of the arch-conservative and partner of the Jesuits, the Austrian Chancellor, Prince Clemens von Metternich. British subsidies made von Gentz the highest paid propagandist in Europe:

...in June 1800, soon after the publication of his Essai sur l'état actuel de l'administration des finances et de la richesse nationale de la Grande Bretagne, *Gentz wrote in his diary 'Through Garlicke, a letter from Lord Grenville, which contains a present ['einem Geschenk'] of £500 – the first of this sort!' ('Garlicke' was a British diplomat, Benjamin Garlike).*[49]

When Benjamin Garlike delivered to Gentz Lord Grenville's letter of June 1800, Gentz promised life-long devotion to "un Souverain, dont j'ai toujours adoré les vertus, la bonté et la sagesse" (a sovereign, whose virtues, goodness and wisdom I have always adored). Between 1806 and 1809 he received £4500 a year [the equivalent of £261,777 in 2005], an enormous sum in those days and "more than an undersecretary of state earned."[50]

In April 1802, following the publication of The State of Europe, *he was able to report in his diary that 'destiny brought a gift ['eine*

Rimesse'] of £1,000 from England!' [the equivlaent of £66,253 in 2005].[51]

He noted that at the Congress of Vienna he received £22,000 [the equivalent of £1,272,488 in 2005] through Talleyrand from the French King Louis XVIII, while his diary, which is full of such entries, says that the British Prime Minister Castlereagh gave him £600, and *'les plus folles promesses.'* Gentz carried on a running battle in European journals against the French propagandist Alexandre d'Hauterive who maintained that Gentz was but an "organ and echo of the English ministry," ... "protected and probably paid" by English gold. This was true. A paid agent of Britain from 1800 onwards, Gentz served as Britain's propagandist, constantly urging the continentals, especially the Austrians and Prussians to unite together against Napoleon and France.

What Gentz was struggling against was the French presentation of themselves as the civilising power of the new Rome, that was seeking to bring order and civilisation to a corrupt Europe they saw as dominated by the selfish neo-Carthaginian piracy of the English. Bertrand Barère, the Toulouse lawyer, presenting a French Navigation Act in September 1793, described England as a "modern Carthage" that had corrupted the world with its "floods of gold" and its *"francisations simulées,"* with its ships sailing under false papers and French flags. The English government was nothing but a global merchant, which "buys and gives prices to men, cities and ports." ... "A ridiculous Anglo-mania" had subjugated France: "commissioners of customs, metal workers, speculators in colonial commodities, shippers of Indian fabrics, these are our real masters." "As a colonial power, it has federalized the globe." In his three-volume work *La liberté des mers* (1798) Barère wrote that the English government spread "anxiety, fear, envy, corruption and hatred;" it had "conceived the project of COLONISING THE UNIVERSE" [emphasis – Barère]; it "divides by words and by things." English law, "in relation to Bengal and to France," was far worse than that of Carthage.[52] Gentz was thus a man whose mind straddled two world views: as an *arriviste* non-aristocrat, he could embrace the coming world of commercial capitalism and global consciousness, but as a bourgeois who wished, like so many of the British middle class would in the coming Victorian era, to enjoy the prestige and privileges of the old aristocracy, he chose to ally himself with the interests of the traditional rulers of European society. A man of his time and a Romantic in his instincts, like so many of the Romantics, from Coleridge and Macauley to Schlegel and Müller, his imagination failed him when it came to social and political affairs, and he fell back into the arms of tradition and order. An immensely talented man, he symbolised in his own career the failure of the spiritual imagination of the European bourgeois in the Napoleonic era.

From 1812, when he became Metternich's secretary and public voice, he was known as 'the Pen of Europe' and was fully involved in the planning and execution of all of Metternich's policies. For the rest of his life, Gentz served Metternich faithfully, castigating liberal democratic movements wherever he found them, and was very active at the various international Congresses overseen by Metternich between 1812 and 1825. His consummate abilities placed him in a secure position among the highest European aristocratic circles. Neither Gentz nor Metternich were religious men; they were interested in preserving the oligarchical conservative order with its privileges for those at the top. Regarding himself to the end of his life as 'a rock of order,' Metternich would have subscribed to the views of his master Emperor Francis I, who said in a speech to professors of a lyceum in Ljubljana in 1821:

> *Keep to the old values: they are good and our ancestors lived well by them, why not we? New ideas now prevail. I cannot approve of them and I will never approve of them. Keep away from them because I do not need scholars, I need good citizens. It is your job to bring up young people for this purpose. Those who serve me must teach what I order. Those who cannot do this or who come with new ideas, they can go, or I will remove them."* [53]

An example of Gentz's intellectual cleverness and long lasting influence is his conservative view of the nature of the American Revolution, which he wished, from his anti-French viewpoint, to contrast with the French Revolution. On this point Luigi Marco Bassani of the rightwing Mises Institute writes:

> *The comparison between the French and the American Revolutions became a favourite pastime for Euro-American intellectuals in the beginning of the 1800's, and it remains quite popular to this day... one of the first of these endeavours was the book written by Friedrich von Gentz... and translated by John Quincy Adams [later US President – TMB], who was at the time, 1800, minister in Berlin.* **Gentz's thesis is important because, articulated for the first time by Burke, it became almost commonplace among scholars for two centuries** *[emphasis – TMB]. The French Revolution was seen as the product of a fanatic zeal for natural rights, the abstract natural rights of mankind, while the American one was viewed instead as a "conservative revolution." The colonists had to break their ties with the mother country because they were claiming the customary rights of Englishmen, while the British Empire was denying to them the status of British subjects. It was thus a revolutionary separation that had very conservative implications: in order to safeguard their juridical and cultural heritage, the Americans were forced to break with the British Empire.*[54]

Gentz argued that Great Britain was the most advanced and modern nation on earth and London a very 'paradise' because of her economic practices and instincts, Britain was politically civilised because she was conservative and ruled by a 'sensible moderate' aristocratic elite.

Gentz's views echoed those of William Pitt, Stanhope's uncle, who in a speech to parliament in 1792 on the 'history of commerce' and the 'constant accumulation of capital' said: "The difficulty will be to imagine limits to its operation. None can be found... while there remains abroad any new market that can be explored, or any existing market that can be extended." Gentz believed that "the advantages of the recent progress of English commerce were 'in a certain sense, and even in a very real sense, assured for ever.'" [55] Gentz presented to his continental readers the new British commercial system as a consequence of mankind's progress: "all civilized nations must be impelled by the desire of establishing a permanent system of connexion with the remotest parts of the world," and "civilization is not to be the exclusive privilege of this or that favoured people; it will spread over the whole habitable globe in the course of time." He argued that English dominance in global commerce was due not to English malpractice and deceit, as his French rival Alexandre d'Hautive argued, but of the "intrinsic, peculiar, positive superiority of the English." [56]

Before moving to Vienna, Gentz had already received his first payment from Lord Grenville of the British Foreign Office government in early 1800. Stanhope's later familiarity with von Gentz on his many visits to the Continent was facilitated by his mother, Louisa Grenville. Not long after moving to Vienna, Gentz was invited to London (August 1802) where he was feted in establishment circles, introduced to King George III, and made much of by Grenville and Pitt, who guaranteed him an annual pension for his continued writings against Napoleon. His path to London was smooth: his translator and go-between was John Charles Herries of the Treasury; his patron in London apparently was William Eden, Lord Auckland, former head of British Intelligence on the Continent. Gentz was a man who would play a key role in the web of destiny linking Stanhope and the western brotherhoods, Kaspar Hauser, Metternich, and the Jesuit-influenced Habsburg court. Ten years before Kaspar Hauser's birth, he took his place in the relationship between Vienna and London, and once Kaspar Hauser was born in 1812, "for ten years, from 1812 onward, Gentz was in closest touch with all the great affairs of European history, the assistant, confidant, and adviser of Metternich. He accompanied the chancellor on all his journeys; was present at all the conferences that preceded and followed the war; no political secrets were hidden from him; and his hand drafted all important diplomatic documents. He was secretary to the congress of Vienna (1814-1815) and to all the congresses and conferences that followed, up to that of Verona (1822)." [57]

He was to maintain his influence until his death, on 9th June 1832, some three months after the death of Goethe; by that time Kaspar Hauser had for six months already been enduring psychological torment in

Ansbach at the household of the teacher Meyer, Stanhope's paid agent, where Stanhope had deposited him. Stanhope's friendship with Gentz began with Stanhope's first visit to Vienna in 1816. It was at that very time that the two men learned from newspaper reports of a mysterious message in a bottle that announced the fact that Kaspar Hauser was being kept near Laufenburg on the Rhine in Southwest Germany. Hauser was moved from there soon after, and then began – presumably at Gentz's request – Stanhope's annual trips to Germany in search of the boy they both feared might become the focus of napoleanic or revolutionary hopes.

Joseph de Maistre

What may well have motivated London to seek to make use of Gentz was Napoleon's appointment as Consul for Life and President of the Italian Republic in January 1802, the point in time, which, according to Rudolf Steiner, indicated the 'cooperative' agreement between Jesuits and Freemasons. As President of the Italian Republic, Napoleon put himself literally on the Pope's doorstep; this was an act which took place against the background of intense negotiations (November 1800-July 1801) between Napoleon's agents and the Vatican for a Concordat between Paris and Rome that would restore the Catholic Church in France to something of its pre-revolution status. The Concordat was signed in July 1801 but first published by Napoleon in April 1802.

> *The French Government by the concordat recognized the Catholic religion as the religion of the great majority of Frenchmen. The phrase was no longer, as in former times, 'the religion of the State.' But it was a question of a personal profession of Catholicism on the part of the Consuls of the Republic. The Holy See had insisted on this mention, and it was only on this condition that the Pope agreed to grant to the State police power in the matter of public worship.*[58]

The Vatican, age-old enemy of the Protestant British state, had thus managed not only to defend Roman Catholicism against the atheistic and secularising forces of the French Revolution, but actually to reconstitute the status of the Faith to a not inconsiderable degree within the revolutionary French state. The *"personal profession of Catholicism on the part of the Consuls of the Republic"* is of particular significance here. Needless to say, within the context of the ongoing centuries-long struggle between the Protestant English establishment and the Vatican and its allies in the Catholic Powers of the Continent, this Concordat was a most unwelcome development. The mainstream among the more radical freemasons in England, including those more involved in both the occult and politics, such as the Duke of Sussex, was a kind of vague pantheistic Deism, infused with rationalist and secularist thought. Both Thomas Jefferson in the United States and Robespierre in France subscribed to spiritual views of this sort. Those English Freemasons who shared such views could have hoped that the French Revolution would spread them in the country that since the time of Clovis (c.500 AD) had often been Rome's most intimate political ally, thus dealing a death blow to the Roman Catholic Church; Catholicism would cease to be a threat to Protestant England. Such hopes appeared to be dashed by Napoleon's Concordat with the Vatican, which meant that the French were once again recognised by the world and by themselves to be spiritual subordinates of the Vatican. Napoleon famously declared his readiness "to make the Pope a present of 30 million French Catholics." He was in effect saying to the Pope: "I shall recognise your spiritual suzerainty over Frenchmen if you make no trouble for my political suzerainty over Europe."

It was in this context that another very significant spiritual subordinate of the Vatican, the Savoyard Count Joseph de Maistre, made a journey to Russia in January 1802.

> *Symbiosis of the extremes of Left and Right is evident in the career of the man who became the leading counter-revolutionary of the era: Joseph de Maistre. As a young and ambitious magistrate, de Maistre became a Mason in 1773 and called for an American Revolution even before the Americans did... De Maistre later confessed that only a radical conversion by the Jesuits kept him "from becoming an orator in the Constituent Assembly." De Maistre took his own positive ideal from the negative portrayal of conservative Catholicism in Germany*

by the revolutionary Mirabeau. Perhaps the two most influential reactionaries of the era were both refugees from the revolutionary occultist infatuations of an earlier period. Karl Eckhartshausen, the leading propagator of the anti-revolutionary mysticism of the "Holy Alliance," was a Bavarian who had briefly joined and subsequently studied at length the Illuminist Order. Joseph de Maistre, the most influential among the unltramontanist breed of reactionary, had been a leader of radical occult Masonry in pre-revolutionary France. ...In one of the last letters which de Maistre received just before his death in 1821, Lamennais... wrote prophetically: 'There will be no more middle way between faith and nothingness... Everything is extreme today; there is no longer any dwelling place in between.' [59]

The later champion of the Pope and the Jesuits did not hesitate as a young Masonic firebrand to enter the lists against a famous Jesuit enemy of Freemasonry – the Abbé Barruel:

Joseph de Maistre, an active freemason and student of mysticism, wrote a long, unpublished refutation of Barruel, exploiting his poor logic and exposing his errors of fact. Later, in his Les Soirées de St Petersbourg *(Lyon, 1874) II pp. 265 ff., he was to attack individual Illuminati for their revolutionary acts but he always excluded mainstream freemasonry from any blame.*[60]

De Maistre was one of those who found it quite easy to move from one side of the spiritual fence to the other – in his case, from radical Freemasonry to ultramontane Catholicism.

From 1774 to 1790 Joseph de Maistre belonged to Masonic lodges in Chambéry and associated with a more esoteric and 'illuminist' brand of Scottish Rite Masons in neighbouring Lyon. This link may appear odd for a future Catholic apologist, but at the time these clubs were often frequented by priests and bishops as well as Catholic noblemen. The lodges were opportune places for an ambitious young man to make friends useful for career advancement and to discuss political reforms. In addition, the mystical doctrines popular in the Masonic circles Maistre frequented appeared to him a providential counter-force to the rationalism and the irreligion of the time.[61]

A Catholic Encyclopaedia entry on Pope Clement XIV, who suppressed the Society of Jesus, notes that:

> *Two non-Catholic sovereigns, Frederick of Prussia and Catherine of Russia, took the Jesuits under their protection. Whatever may have been their motives... their intervention kept the order alive until its complete restoration in 1804* [actually, 1814 – TMB] *...The Jesuits retained possession of all their colleges and of the University of Breslau until 1806 and 1811, but they ranked as secular priests and admitted no more novices. But Catherine II resisted to the end. By her order the bishops of White Russia ignored the Brief of suppression and commanded the Jesuits to continue to live in communities and go on with their usual work. Clement XIV seems to have approved of their conduct.*
>
> *Frederick, by preserving the Jesuits in his dominions, rendered the Church a good, though perhaps unintended, service. He also authorized the erection of a Catholic church in Berlin.*[62]

The Jesuits were masters at infiltrating organizations and cultures; they had been doing it for centuries, even in the Far East, so insinuating themselves into Protestant and Masonic groups was no great challenge to them. They knew how to immerse themselves in the company of their enemies in order to become like them.

De Maistre was not exactly an example of the phenomenon quoted above to which Steiner was referring in 1916,[63] but he was one of the many who were more than familiar with both camps, and who moved from one to the other, rather in the manner of the American Neo-cons today who started out as liberal Democrats in the 60's and 70's and have ended up as equally radical conservatives. De Maistre, however, deserves special mention because he was a one-off, an especially talented spiritual campaigner whose influence spread far and wide throughout the 19th century. In April 1802, the very year to which Steiner drew attention, von Gentz, the cynical self-seeker, former Mason and libertine, and de Maistre, also former Mason and now champion of the Pope, actually met – at the house of an English diplomat!

> *Gentz reported in his diary in April 1802 that he had dinner in Berlin, at the house of an English diplomat, with the 'great Count Maistre,' on his way 'from Turin to Petersburg.'* [64]

This diplomat could well have been Francis Jackson, secretary to the British legation at the time, a friend both to William Pitt and to Philip Henry Stanhope. Jackson had enabled Stanhope to escape from his tyrannical father, the 3rd Earl, and go to Germany to study. Jackson had also been a rival of Gentz for the love of the same woman, and the two men had become firm friends. This friendship would later lead Stanhope to Vienna.

Adam Czartoryski

As a citizen of Savoy, de Maistre fled to the neighbouring Kingdom of Piedmont and Sardinia when the French invaded his homeland; thus, when the French revolutionaries, many of whom had been inspired by Illuminist Masonic ideals, invaded Savoy, the Savoyard champion of Jesuitism and the Catholic Church, who had also been associating with Illuminist Freemasons, left for Russia, one of the two countries (the other being Lutheran Prussia) where the Jesuits had regrouped following the abolition of their Order by their own monarch, the Pope. In 1783 there were 72 members of the Society of Jesus in Russia; by 1805 their number had risen to 280 and by the time of their expulsion from Russia in 1820 there were 358 Jesuits in the Empire.[65] In Sardinia de Maistre had been appointed ambassador to Russia after having made the acquaintance in 1801 of Adam Czartoryski (1770-1861), a Polish nobleman who was one of Czar Alexander I's closest advisers and also the decades-long lover of the Czar's wife! **She happened to be Luisa von Baden** (1770-1826), *sister of Karl von Baden and thus Kaspar Hauser's aunt.* In his book *Lord Stanhope – Der Gegenspieler Kaspar Hausers,*[66] the Kaspar Hauser researcher Johannes Mayer presents documentary evidence which shows that Czar Alexander, through his connections to the Beauharnais family, was already in 1814 aware of the fate that had befallen Kaspar Hauser and was doing all he could to protect the interests of the Beauharnais.

In 1789 Czartoryski had visited England and attended the sensational trial of Warren Hastings. During his second visit in 1793 he made connections with many of the English aristocracy and studied the English constitution. He became a leading Freemason with close links to leading British Freemasons, notably Frederick Augustus, the Duke of Sussex (Grand Master of British Freemasonry, 1813-1843). Czartoryski's friend, Emperor Alexander I, a liberal and a Masonic fellow traveller, appointed Peter Vasilevich Zavadovsky, a pupil of the Jesuits, to be his minister of education.

> *...from the beginning of 1804... [Czartoryski] had the practical control of Russian diplomacy. His first act was to protest energetically against the murder of the duc d'Enghien (20th March 1804), and insist on an immediate rupture with France... on the 9th of August a note dictated by Czartoryski to Alexander was sent to the Russian minister in London, urging the formation of an anti-French coalition. It was Czartoryski also who framed the Convention of the 6th of November 1804, whereby Russia agreed to put 115,000 and Austria 235,000 men in the field against Napoleon. Finally, on the 11th of April 1805 he signed an offensive-defensive alliance with England. But his most striking ministerial act was a memorial written in 1805, but otherwise undated, which aimed at transforming the whole map of Europe. In brief it amounted to this: Austria and Prussia were to divide Germany between them. Russia was to acquire the Dardanelles, the Sea of Marmora, the Bosphorus with Constantinople, and Corfu. Austria was to have Bosnia, Wallachia and Ragusa. Montenegro, enlarged by Mostar and the Ionian Islands, was to form a separate state. England and Russia together were to maintain the equilibrium of the world. In return for their acquisitions in Germany, Austria and Prussia were to consent to the erection of an autonomous Polish state extending from Danzig to the sources of the Vistula, under the protection of Russia. Fantastic as*

it was in some particulars, this project was partly realized in more recent times... [in 1810] Czartoryski quitted St Petersburg for ever; but the personal relations between him and Alexander were never better. The friends met again at Kalisch shortly before the signature of the Russo-Prussian alliance of the 20th of February 1813, and Czartoryski was in the emperor's suite at Paris in 1814, and rendered his sovereign material services at the congress of Vienna.[67]

After 1815, in Russia, Czartoryski was to represent the anti-Russian and anti-Austrian interests of the British oligarchy, in line with those interests sought to promote Slav nationalism. His schemes, notably those he hatched while residing in exile at the Hotel Lambert in Paris during the last 30 years of his life, were to lay the foundations for the dreams of a Greater Serbia that fuelled the fanaticism of Serbian nationalists and reached their catastrophic climax a hundred years later in the summer of 1914.

Czartoryski's biographer Marian Kukiel, director of many years standing of the Cracow Czartoryski Archive, mentions... further that the design of the Pole-in-exile corresponded to a large extent to the map of Europe rearranged in 1919 through the Paris peace treaties, while his nationality concept seems like a blueprint of Wilson's catchword of 'self-determination of nations.' In addition, Kukiel discreetly indicates that the two Western powers [France and Britain] would first have to win over Russia for Czartoryski's arrangement, having first of all to transform the entente cordiale into a triple entente for this purpose – the constellation that existed on the eve of the first world war. This Balkan Federation, guided by the West, was to eliminate, to a large extent, the Central European (Habsburg) influence in this territory, and above all, the spiritual and cultural one.[68]

These two men, the Savoyard Joseph de Maistre and the Polish nobleman Prince Adam Czartoryski, who met in Sardinia and cooperated in Russia, were of the kind that moved with ease in Freemasonic and Jesuit circles. Both Czartoryski's father and Metternich were members of the exclusive and ancient Order of the Knights of the Golden Fleece – the epitome of Catholic aristocracy, although Metternich himself does not seem to have been a particularly ardent Catholic. Metternich's father, Franz Georg Karl von Metternich (1746-1818) is known to have been a member of Adam Weishaupt's Illuminati Order: his codename was Ximenez. As with the third and fourth Earls Stanhope, the Metternich father and son had differing political views. De Maistre, however, put his brilliant writings at the service of the absolute authority of the Vatican, and Rudolf Steiner, who had much to say about him in a lecture of 1st May 1921,[69] acknowledged him to be "a personality of the greatest imaginable genius" and "the finest and most brilliant representative of what infused France from Romanism," but who nevertheless represented the "obsolete archaic light of Ormuzd" in its continuing age-old battle with Ahriman, the demonic element that de Maistre saw in the modern form of British culture, especially since the time of Francis Bacon and John Locke. Czartoryski, on the other hand, a close personal friend of both the Whig politicians Grey and Brougham, later members of Palmerston's cabinet, who were both very friendly to the Poles, worked in the service of those western brotherhoods whose secretive methods of working Steiner depicts in such detail in his lectures of the winter of 1916-1917,[70] and who sought to make use of Slavic nationalism in order to destroy the spiritual impulses of Central Europe.

> *Czartoryski... argued that independent Slavic states should be created in the Balkans under Russian protection. Serbia "should be the legitimate banner of all South Slavs, the centre around which all others should gather." He had contact with Ilija Gerasanin, an influential Serbian statesman, who he advised to rely on Britain to achieve national unity and independence. Russia and Austria were to be avoided "because the patron might become easily the master." Czartoryski was apprehensive of Russian dominance and imperialist expansion in the Balkans under the cover of Pan-Slavism. He advised Gerasanin to establish secret societies in the South Slav provinces under the control of poverenici ('men of trust') who would organize when the Ottoman Empire collapsed. In 1844, Gerasanin published*

Nacertanije *which outlined his position on foreign policy. He envisioned unity only of Serbs, a Pan-Serbian nationalism, that would unite all the Serbian Orthodox populations of the Balkans into a single state. His focus was on Bosnia-Hercegovina which he sought to incorporate into a Pan-Serbian state, a Greater Serbian state. Moreover, Gerasanin maintained that an alliance was possible with Russia against the Ottoman Empire and Austria.*[71]

In his Twilight Hours in St Petersburg (1821), de Maistre writes of the "dreadful seeds" of Locke's philosophy which "perhaps would not have come to fruition under the ice of his style" but that "animated in the hot mud of Paris, they have produced the monster of the Revolution that has engulfed Europe." [72]

Gentz, de Maistre and Czartoryski, as representatives of Central, Western and Eastern Europe, were key figures who can be counted as among the opponents of the spiritual stream of Kaspar Hauser, although in the case of de Maistre and Czartoryski there is no evidence that they were in any way directly connected with the bid to destroy him. None of them had any understanding of the positive cultural role of Central Europe and worked only for their own special interests. De Maistre, the thinker, cared only for the authority and glory of the Papacy and the Roman Church; he was an internationalist in the Jesuit sense and at a time when the Jesuit cause appeared very much to be on the ropes, he was the man who took up their sword in defence of the Papacy. Czartoryski, the man of action, was a Polish Catholic nationalist who, in order to restore his nation to its former glories, was prepared to reshape the rest of Europe and cast it into conflagration – the proponent of the poisonous brew of Pan-Slavism that would ultimately be the instrument of Central Europe's destruction and the bipolar division of the Continent in 1945. Gentz, the mercurial penman, propagandist and amoral libertine who lived on his wits, moved from radicalism to arch-reaction in Metternich's service. He introduced to Metternich the British concept of the Balance of Power, which until 1820 the British and Austrian governments sought to manipulate in order to frustrate the aims of Russia and Prussia.

These three men revolved around three even greater personalities who could arguably be said to have been, apart from the phenomenon of Napoleon Bonaparte, the prime movers and shakers of events in the first 33 years of the nineteenth century – on the visible stage of events at least: Prince Clemens von Metternich, Chancellor of Austria, who, while not a Jesuit himself, stood as the champion of the House of Habsburg that since the 16th century had been the stalwart bastion of Papal supremacy and the upholder of a backward-looking, Catholic, mediaeval, European Christendom; Nathan Rothschild, the Jewish banker, internationalist and cosmopolitan, who saw in money and finance the real powers of the future; Augustus Frederick, the Duke of Sussex and Grand Master of British Freemasonry 1813-1843, an aristocrat with a consuming passion for Jewish and Egyptian esotericism, who stood close to the moneyed leaders of the British establishment and represented the traditional Whig landed aristocracy that had ruled Britain since 'the Glorious Revolution' of 1688 and which was, despite the rise of capitalism in Britain, determined to maintain its grip on power by the use of occult means where necessary.

The Duke of Sussex

Augustus Frederick, the Duke of Sussex (1773-1843), sixth son of George III, was known amongst other things for his closeness to and patronage of the Jewish community in London. The *Jewish Daily Post*, 6th May 1935, states "The Duke of Sussex was an open friend of the Jewish community... he opened his doors to Jews with great affability." The wealthy Goldsmid brothers, leading figures in London's Jewish community, were on very intimate terms with the Royal Dukes, the sons of George III, who enjoyed their company and their hospitality. So keen was the young Duke to associate with the rich of the Jewish community, learn what he could from them, and gain their support that on one occasion, he drove back from Abraham Goldsmid's house at Morden disguised for the journey as a distinguished foreigner in a carriage with Hymon the famous pastry-cook. In association with the House of Baring, Abraham Goldsmid contracted in 1810 for the Government Loan of

£14,000,000. At a great party on 14th April 1809 at the Great Synagogue in the appropriately named Duke's Place, St James's, new hangings of crimson velvet within the sacred precincts attracted attention. They had been presented for the occasion by one Nathan Mayer Rothschild, the rising young financier not long since arrived in London from Frankfurt via Manchester, and already well known in financial circles. In attendance was the Duke of Sussex, later to make himself known as a student of Hebrew and champion of Jewish rights.

> *Yesterday, at half past six o'clock, the Dukes of Cumberland, Sussex and Cambridge attended the Great Synagogue in Duke's Place to witness the Hebrew form of worship. The preparation made to receive the princes evidenced the loyalty of the Jewish people, and the spectacle was magnificent and most solemn. The Synagogue was most suitably decorated on the occasion. The seats on each side were raised and the pulpit in the centre was adorned by crimson and gold. A space between the pulpit and the ark was appropriated to the Royal Dukes and the Nobility, who stood on a rich platform with four beautiful Egyptian chairs and stands for their books, flowers, etc. The Synagogue was brilliantly illuminated by chandeliers. The High Priest, Rabbi Hirschell, in his sacerdotal habit displayed unusual magnificence: he was dressed in a robe of white satin of considerable value and ordered expressly for him by Abraham Goldsmid, Esq. The Royal Dukes arrived in the carriage of Mr. Goldsmid, and their own carriages followed with several ladies of distinction. The singing was excellent and the Royal Dukes appeared much gratified by the Choruses. When the Ark was opened to take out the Five Books of Moses the Princes were conducted by Mr. Goldsmid to view the interior, at which they expressed great satisfaction, the structure being grand and beautiful. The galleries were crowded with beautiful Jewesses who attracted much the attention of the Royal Party. After the service, the Royal Dukes drove to the mansion of Mr. A. Goldsmid, where a sumptuous entertainment was provided, which was followed by a grand concert.*
>
> *About 1840, the Duke of Sussex commissioned a portrait of*

himself for the Jews' Hospital. On attending the Duke at Kensington Palace, the Jewish painter Solomon Hart, was surprised to find that the Duke knew all about him. 'You forget,' said the Duke, 'the peculiarity which distinguishes my family. We collect a quantity of information and facts concerning persons and their affairs which we never forget. I know when you lived in Newcastle Street, Strand, over the milk shop where you struggled all day to get bread for certain members of your family whom you supported, and when you could only afford time in the evenings to pursue your studies at the R.A.[73]

In his activity as a leading Freemason, the Duke was very drawn to Cabbalistic studies. Freemasonic ritual was, after all, based largely on the esotericism of the Temple of Solomon and rooted in Jewish culture and language. His lifelong interest in Hebrew and biblical studies apparently began during his student years at Göttingen University in Germany. In this context, the following observation is of interest:

...in the German press [Adam Smith's book Wealth of Nations] was neither quoted nor confuted, but merely ignored; and... Smith's name was very seldom mentioned, and then without any idea of his importance. One spot ought to be excepted – the little kingdom of Hanover, which, from its connection with the English Crown, participated in the contemporary French complaint of Anglomania. Göttingen had its influential school of admirers of English institutions and literature; the 'Wealth of Nations' was reviewed in the Gelehrte Anzeigen *of Gottingen early in 1777, and one of the professors of the University there announced a course of lectures upon it in the winter session of 1777-78.*[74]

The Duke, known as 'the Philo-Semite,' had been a good friend of the eccentric Lord George Gordon (1751-1793), a convert to Judaism and a hater of the Bourbons, who ended his days in Newgate Prison where he was frequently visited by his friends the royal Dukes of York, Clarence and Sussex, Freemasons all. As a young man the Duke of Sussex had been close to Sir William Hamilton (1730-1803), husband of Emma Hamilton (later Nelson's mistress) who had done much research in Italy into vulcanology and the surviving cult of priapism, which his huge collection of antique classical vases did much to popularise among the chattering classes of 18th century England. From these circles emerged the interest in rediscovering pagan ideas of the role of sex in religion and ritual, the phallus as symbol of the creative regenerative principle of the universe, and the female organs as the symbol of the cosmos. Oriental cosmogonies too that suggested a 'cosmic sexuality' were at this time beginning to make their way into the European mind as a result of mercantile, imperial, and missionarising impulses. These oriental ideas included that of the cosmic Yin and Yang from China, and Tantric ideas from India.

Into this swirling intellectual ferment of the mid-to-late eighteenth century, this semi-rationalist, sentimental atmosphere of yearning for a lost age of sexual innocence and play, came the somewhat more ambiguous element of Jewish Sabbatean sex magic via Samuel Falk (c.1710-1782), a Master of practical Cabbalistic magic, who arrived in London in 1742. Like the Jesuits, the crypto-Sabbatean followers of Falk were practised in the art of deception and dissembling. They held it acceptable to mix in among their enemies and adopt their ways, even to the extent of standing normal morality on its head; their behaviour was deeply repugnant to orthodox Jews, who regarded all followers of the 17th century false Messiah Sabbatai Zevi as heretics. Some have argued that both Cagliostro, and less convincingly, Swedenborg, learned something from Falk and his community of highly unorthodox Jews, notably in the area of sexuality and free love. There is also evidence to suggest that it was Falk who stimulated Cagliostro to go to Egypt and bring his pseudo-Egyptian esotericism into European Freemasonry. It was Cagliostro who specialised in using young people and children as mediums and channellers, something that Stanhope and Edward Bulwer Lytton would be much engaged in some 50 years later and which may also have interested them in Kaspar Hauser. One of the most significant of those who learned from Falk was the richest man in France, the Duke d'Orleans, Louis Phillippe (later Citizen Égalité) 1747-1793, a close friend of the Prince of Wales (later King George IV, 1820-1830). The Duke, installed as first Grand Master of the atheistic Grand Orient lodge

on 23rd October 1773, was deeply involved in the preparation that led to
the French Revolution of 1789, voted for the execution of his cousin King
Louis and was himself eventually guillotined in 1793; his son was to
become King Louis-Phillippe in the French Revolution of 1830. "The
whole Orleans family, ever since Phillippe's great-grandfather the Regent,
was notoriously involved in the black arts." [75]

Samuel Falk was rebuffed by the Jewish community of London
until he was accepted and supported by Aaron Goldsmid, founder of the
distinguished family of financiers, who became his spiritual follower and
the eventual executor of his will. During the lifetime of Aaron's sons,

> *...familiarity with the sons of George III did much to break down
> social prejudice against Jews in England and to pave the way for
> emancipation. They were considered by Lord Nelson among his
> closest friends... This activity marked the displacement of the
> Sephardi element in London from their former hegemony...
> Benjamin was... the founder of the Naval Asylum, Greenwich, and,
> in 1797, of the Jews' Hospital, Mile End. A favourite of both Pitt and
> the Duke of Kent... in 1808, in a fit of despondency, Benjamin
> Goldsmid committed suicide. [His brother Abraham also killed
> himself two years later – TMB]. Lord Nelson was among their closest
> friends. He spent his last night in England in Benjamin's house at
> Roehampton.* [76]

Through the Goldsmids at least, and probably through his own
contacts as well, the Duke of Sussex was in close touch with the Falk
stream of magical Sabbateanism. He did all he could to aid Jewish
Freemasons, most notably those in Frankfurt, the home of the Rothschilds
and a town which would later figure on almost all of Stanhope's many
trips to Germany in connection with Kaspar Hauser. In England, Nathan
Rothschild, who was initiated on 24th October 1802 in Emulation Lodge
No. 12, London, recognised, as did all other 'Modern' Freemasons, the
Duke of Sussex as his Grand Master. [77]

> *In a number of German Lodges the masonic reforms then gradually
> began to have the effect of dismissing the problem of creed, and, in*

proportion as the Lodges re-approached the original English conception, the idea of tolerance regained the character it had in the minds of the founders of the London Grand Lodge. A very interesting situation was created when the Grand Lodge of England, acting contrary to the view of its Provincial Grand Lodge in Frankfurt, now granted a Charter to the 'Nascent Dawn' Lodge, which had seceded from the Grand Orient of France for political reasons. During the discussion, it expressed its wish once again that the 'universal religion' should suffer no restraint. The Grand Master, the Duke of Sussex... expressed himself to German Freemasons with extraordinary clarity..." The Grand Master impressed upon the delegates of the 'Nascent Dawn' Lodge that:

"Not only in Frankfurt but in the whole of Germany do I want to make an Epoch with this Constitution, for I perceive that instead of making progress there, enlightenment is on the decline. I do not ask whether this Constitution pleases the other Lodges very much... The other Lodges have certainly no cause to be ashamed of what the Grand Lodge of England, the first Mother Lodge of all, recognizes." [78]

Both in Germany and England rich Jewish families had by this time become key cultural elements in their respective societies:

They are by far the richest non-noble families in this city, and almost the only ones that receive company, and in whose circle, owing to their numerous foreign connections, you may meet strangers of all ranks; therefore, whoever likes to mix in good society without much ceremony, gets introduced to these families. [79]

Niall Ferguson says his colossal study of the Rothschilds:

...the speed with which Mayer Amschel's wealth grew in the 1790's marked a real break with his earlier business activity. At the beginning of the 1790's Mayer Amschel Rothschild was no more than a prosperous antique-dealer. By 1797 he was one of the richest Jews in Frankfurt, and a central part of his business was unmistakably

*banking. The evidence for this breakthrough is unequivocal. In 1795
the official figure for Mayer Amschel's taxable wealth was doubled to
4,000 gulden; a year later he was moved into the top tax bracket, with
property worth more than 15,000 gulden; and in the same year he
was listed as the tenth richest man in the Judengasse with taxable
wealth of over 60,000 gulden. Thanks largely to Mayer Amschel, the
Rothschilds had become one of the eleven richest families in the
Judengasse by 1800.* [80]

A key role in the later rise to prominence of the Rothschilds, as in
that of Friedrich von Gentz (noted above), was played by British
government Treasury official John Charles Herries:

*In 1830, a proposal was made by the Government to the East India
Company for the reduction of its dividends; the Rothschilds, who had
£40,000 of East India stock, sold it all out. Undoubtedly it was Rt.
Hon. J. C. Herries, then in the Cabinet as Master of the Mint and
President of the Board of Trade, who gave the Rothschilds notice of the
intended change. (K, letter 9th Jan.uary 1830). Herries had always
been hand-in-glove with Nathan ever since he had been comptroller
of accounts in the Napoleonic Wars. (It is significant that Herries' son
was made Chairman of the Board of Revenue by Disraeli in 1877).* [81]

No mere official, the staunchly reactionary tory John Charles
Herries was later appointed to almost all the major posts of government:
Secretary to the Treasury (1823-1827), Chancellor of the Exchequer in
Lord Goderich's government (1827-1828), Master of the Mint under the
Duke of Wellington (1828-1830), briefly President of the Board of Trade
(1830), Secretary of War under Sir Robert Peel (1834-1835), and finally
President of the Board of Control in Lord Derby's first government
(1852). He was also a defeated rival of Disraeli for the leadership of the
Conservative Party, ironic in view of his work for the Rothschilds, without
whose help Disraeli would have been unable to rise as far as he did.

*John Charles Herries, (1778-1855) army commissary and financier...
became private secretary to prime minister Spencer Perceval before*

being placed in 1811 as army commissary-in-chief to act against 'the
contractors.' Information is contradictory on whether John Charles
was connected with the bank, Herries-Farquhar; one would think, he
was not directly connected. Kynaston, City of London, p. 54,
discusses John Charles' links to the banker N.M. Rothschild.[82]

Nathan had the right connections. Shortly after
N.M.Rothschild opened for business in London, a certain John
Charles Herries was appointed superintendent of the Treasury.
Herries was well-disposed towards Nathan Rothschild not only
because he could fulfil his own ambition – Herries was himself the
son of a minor banker and had had a rapid rise at the Treasury – but
because he also had a weakness for Germany [emphasis – TMB]
and thus became Nathan's first friend in an influential position.[83]

Niall Ferguson notes that Herries had studied in Leipzig in his
youth and had most likely fathered an illegitimate child there by the wife
of one Baron Limburger, a tobacco merchant, who later claimed to have
introduced him to Nathan Rothschild. Certainly, Rothschild would later
have reason to be thankful to Herries, who opened up government
business to him. By the year of Kaspar Hauser's death in 1833, Nathan
Rothschild was master of all he surveyed, arguably the most powerful man
in Europe, the man who was literally enabling the new world to happen as
his bank and his family financed the mushrooming spidery growth of the
world's first 'Internet,' the railway network. He cared not a jot for
traditional niceties, and instead saw through to the reality of the modern
world, famously declaring: "I care not what puppet is placed upon the
throne of England to rule the Empire on which the sun never sets. The
man who controls Britain's money supply controls the British Empire, and
I control the British money supply."

In his *Biographical Notes on the House of Rothschild,* Friedrich von
Gentz praised Mayer Amschel, adding: "Nevertheless, the most
outstanding personal qualities may sometimes require exceptional
circumstances and world-shattering events to come to fruition." Those
circumstances were the French Revolution and the emergence of
Napoleon. The man Rothschild helped destroy, Napoleon Bonaparte (the

Rothschilds financed the 1815 campaign against Napoleon that ended at Waterloo), wanted a France that was free from the power of banks and national debt; he said: "The hand that gives is above the hand that takes. Money has no motherland; financiers are without patriotism and without decency: their sole object is gain."

The Berlin League of Virtue or Tugenbund often held its meetings at the home of Dr. Marcus Herz, friend and pupil of Moses Mendelssohn, the well-known Jewish radical 'intellectual:'

> *The Tugendbund or Virtuous Circle, used to meet in the house of the Jewish doctor, Dr.Marcus Herz; the focal point of the circle was his wife, Henriette...*[84]

The most significant member of the earlier 'culturally oriented' Tugendbund was Friedrich von Gentz, who had been a pupil of Kant's at Königsberg. According to the *Jewish Chronicle,* 1st September 1922, Mrs. Herz herself said that the Tugendbund Jews keenly supported the French Revolution. Although Mayer Amschel Rothschild, father of the famous five sons cannot be said to have supported the Illuminati, members of his family had close relations with some of the members of the Tugendbund. In 1807, a second Tugendbund was established, its aim being nothing less than the forging of a united Germany against Napoleon; Amschel Rothschild stood close to it, and "the Rothschilds appear to have become members." [85] William of Hesse-Cassel was an important member, and the Rothschilds acted as go-betweens for his correspondence concerning it and made payments in favour of the Tugendbund... It was von Gentz to whom the Rothschilds owed their later position with Prince Metternich of Austria.[86] Gentz first met the Rothschilds in 1818, and therafter accepted many 'donations' from them for services rendered as their publicist and media watchdog; he used his vast influence and political weight as Metternich's 'Pen of Europe' to make sure no unduly negative reports appeared in the continental media about the family. In 1826 he even wrote the first official (eulogistic) *Brockhaus* encyclopedia entry about the family.

The year 1801 deserves mention for two other events that occurred far distant from each other. The Rite of Misraim first appeared in Venice in 1801, "according to Bedarride, and was largely the work of Baron Tassoni [whose] work was seen as a revival of previous Egyptian themes and was a continuation of the work started by Parenti. This early incarnation of the Rite of Misraim did not contain more than twenty degrees." [87] Here then, we see a recurrence of the atavistic Egyptian theme which from this time on would become ever stronger in western culture, eventually replacing the Greco-Roman stylistic heritage of the previous 300 years until in the 20th century it would come to dominate western society in the monumental grotesqueness of modernist architecture and the soulless groupthink mindset of elite-ruled totalitarian societies. The atavistic hierarchical element was further developed across the Atlantic, when on 31st May 1801 in Charleston, South Carolina, the Supreme Council was established above the 33 degrees of the Ancient and Accepted Scottish Rite of Freemasonry. "The first two members of the Supreme Council were Colonel John Mitchell, an officer in the Army of the United States in the War of the Revolution, and Dr. Frederick Dalcho, [then a medical doctor] and later clergyman of the Church of England." [88]

This mention of America inevitably leads to another epoch-making event of these years – the Louisiana Purchase of 1803. More than 2 million sq. km. (800,000 sq. mi.) of land extending from the Mississippi River to the Rocky Mountains and from the Gulf of Mexico to the Canadian border. The price was 60 million francs, about $15 million (less than 5 cents an acre!); $11,250,000 was to be paid directly, with the balance to be covered by the assumption by the United States of French debts to American citizens. At the time of the sale the Americans had not yet even begun to fully penetrate the lands they claimed between the original 13 colonies and the Mississippi.

The world-historical significance of this 'commercial' deal cannot be overestimated. The Louisiana Purchase ensured the victory of English-speaking people on the North American continent and thus the eventual dominance of the USA, the megastate of the western world, which, with that other continental empire, Russia, would between them squeeze Germany and Europe in a vice-like grip, ultimately symbolised by the meeting of US and Russian troops on the Elbe in 1945 and the subsequent division of Germany and Europe. It was the vast rich prairie lands west of the Mississippi that would, in the first half of the 19th century and via the port of New Orleans, help provide the financial wherewithal to fund the USA's industrial take-off in the second half of the century. In the Louisiana Purchase too, the impulsive Napoleon played the decisive, though short-sighted, role. It is remarkable to think that an English bank, Barings, lent the more farsighted Thomas Jefferson the money to pay Napoleon for the Purchase, which he then used to kill the soldiers and sailors of Britain and its allies; only 20 years before, the American colonial rebels themselves had been killing British troops in their thousands. Alexander Baring, of Hope and Baring, British bankers, travelled to Paris for talks with the French Minister Barbé Marbois, *even after war between their countries had been declared.* Then Baring went to America, collected the bonds himself and took them back to England. Napoleon thus received his $11 million dollars for his next war against Britain. Thomas Jefferson had presciently written in April 1802:

> *This little event, of France's possessing herself of Louisiana... is the embryo of a tornado which will burst on the countries on both sides of the Atlantic and involve in its effects their highest destinies.*

Napoleon – also with some prescience – said of the Purchase:

> *This accession of territory strengthens forever the power of the United States; and I have just given to England a maritime rival that will, sooner or later, humble her pride.*

It is not without significance perhaps that the years 1995 and 2005 saw the destruction of both Barings Bank, by one man (rogue trader Nick Leeson), and New Orleans, by a force of nature (hurricane Katrina).

Summary

Kaspar Hauser, then, incarnated into a decisive period of world history in which the 20th and 21st centuries were being prepared: the French Revolution and its manifold, mostly baleful effects on social developments, the Napoleonic comet, the discovery of electricity and Uranus, the burgeoning development of the Industrial Revolution, the birth of the German Romantic and nationalist movements, the emergence of the American and Russian titans onto the world stage together with the titanic music of Beethoven sounding out from Central Europe, the tragic initiation of China into the modern world by Britain with the start of the modern international drugs trade, and the beginning of the end of slavery. Kaspar Hauser's spiritual enemies may well have known of his coming and of the danger that he posed to the eventual appearance of their own master – Ahriman. A way had to be found to blunt his impulse or destroy it altogether. Friedrich von Gentz proved to be a central figure in this endeavour; his own destiny and influential connections took him seamlessly from one oligarchical grouping to another – from the Protestant Masonic circles of Prussia and England to the archconservative aristocratic ones of Catholic Austria in the service of Prince Metternich. Threads led too between Gentz and the Rothschilds and their friend, the Duke of Sussex. All these figures represented elitist forces from the past that sought to preserve the hold of different types of oligarchy on the peoples of Europe after the fall of Napoleon – overt and violent in Metternich's area of influence; deceptive and manipulative under the control of the Rothschilds and the British political classes. The Child of Europe, acting as leader of a united Greater German Confederation in the middle of the continent would, by the time of his maturity in mid-century (36 years old in 1848), have been a most potent threat to these forces of manipulation and repression. Let us recall Steiner's words quoted earlier by Ludwig Polzer Hoditz:

But that was not wanted by those circles (the western lodges and the Jesuits). They could not tolerate a centre that was awakening to consciousness if they were not to relinquish their power and designs for power. A spirit such as Goethe's frightened them.

Kaspar Hauser's Allies Beyond Nuremberg

Much has been written about the wonderful group of seven individualities whom destiny brought to Kaspar Hauser in Nuremberg in his first 3 years there: the jailer Hiltel, Dr. Preu, Mayor Binder, Professor Daumer, Court President Anselm von Feuerbach, Baron von Tucher, and also Pastor Fuhrmann from Ansbach.[89] That will not be repeated here. Instead, we shall consider some of those great individualities, contemporaries of Kaspar Hauser, who can be associated with his impulse and what he did for Europe and the world.

Rudolf Steiner made clear that the supersensible School of Michael came to an end in the late 18th century and culminated with what he called the Cosmic Cultus in which Michael prepared his pupils and servants for his own change in status, which would occur approximately a century later, in 1879. He would not only become once more the Regent of the Age, the Time Spirit of the period 1879 to c.2233 (he had been Regent before, from c.600 to c.200 BC); with this new Regency he would also begin his ascent from the archangelic realm to that of the Archai, the Spirits of Personality. These are beings whose rulership lasts for 2160 years and who mediate zodiacal impulses down to mankind over the whole globe. Michael's assumption of his Regency would begin by a harrowing of the heavens in which ahrimanic beings were to be ejected from the supersensible Moon sphere and forced down into the supersensible sphere of Man on Earth, namely, into the human thought world. Steiner puts it like this:

> *An intense will was present in the spiritual life of Europe to take a strong hold of thoughts. In the realms above the Earth these happenings led, at the beginning of the 19th century, to a great far-reaching Act in the spiritual world and what was later on to become Anthroposophy on the earth was cast into mighty Imaginations. In the first half of the 19th century, and even for a short period at the end of the 18th, those who had been Platonists under the teachers of Chartres, who were now living between death and rebirth, and those who had established Aristotelianism on earth and who long ago*

passed through the gate of death – all of them were reunited in the heavenly realms in a great super-earthly Cult or Ritual. Through this Act all that in the 20th century was to be spiritually established as the new Christianity after the beginning of the new Michael Age in the last third of the 19th century – all this was cast into mighty Imaginations... Up above, in the spiritual world, in mighty cosmic Imaginations, preparation was made for that creation of the Intelligence – an entirely spiritual creation – which was then to come forth as Anthroposophy. What trickled through made a very definite impression upon Goethe... he elaborated these little miniature pictures in his Fairy Tale of the Green Snake and the Beautiful Lily ...at the turn of the 18th century (1795)... Having lived in the super-earthly realms in Imaginative form, Anthroposophy was to come down to the earth... At the end of the 18th and the beginning of the 19th centuries it is in very truth a heavenly Anthroposophical Movement... But it was to come down in the real sense in the last third of the 19th century.[90]

Out of this 'heavenly Anthroposophy' the individuality Kaspar Hauser descended to his earthly mission in Central Europe:

South Germany should have become the new Grail Castle of the new Knights of the Grail and the cradle of future events. This spiritual ground had been well-prepared by all those personalities whom we know of as Goethe, Schiller, Hölderlin, Herder and others Kaspar Hauser was to have gathered around him, as it were, all that existed in this spiritual ground thus prepared.[91]

To gain a further insight into Kaspar's origins, let us look in more detail at one of the greatest of these personalities, contemporary with Kaspar Hauser, to whom something of the content of 'the heavenly Anthroposophy' descended: the great philosopher Georg Wilhelm Friedrich Hegel (1770-1831).

Often called the quintessentially German philosopher, the mystic of ideas who freely acknowledged his debt to the Rosicrucian Jacob Boehme, Georg Wilhelm Friedrich Hegel was born in Stuttgart on

27th August 1770. His destiny connected him to Kaspar Hauser's circle, albeit indirectly. Hegel's life, with the exception of his years in Jena and Berlin, was lived almost entirely in the same southern region as that of Kaspar Hauser. He entered the University of Tübingen in 1788 where he developed friendships with the poet Friedrich Hölderlin and the philosopher Friedrich Wilhelm Joseph von Schelling. Hegel went on from there to Berne, where he became in 1793 a private tutor. In Frankfurt from 1797 to 1801, and in Jena until 1806, he was forced by French invasion to flee to Nuremberg, where he worked as a much respected teacher at the Royal Grammar School until 1816. It was in Nuremberg that he settled down, became a family man, marrying Marie von Tucher (16th September 1811), the sister of Gottlieb, Baron von Tucher (1798-1877), who would become Kaspar Hauser's guardian. It turned out to be a blissfully happy marriage, blessed with several children. Another in the charmed circle of men who acted as the protectors of Kaspar Hauser in Nuremberg was Friedrich Daumer, described by Rudolf Steiner as 'the last Rosicrucian.' He was not only a pupil of Hegel's at the Grammar School, but was also a tutor to Hegel's children. While at Nuremberg, Hegel published over a period of several years *The Science of Logic*,[92] a book the ideas of which, Rudolf Steiner claimed, had been wrested by force from Ahriman and placed at the service of Man. From Nuremberg Hegel moved on to a professorship in philosophy at the University of Heidelberg and then in 1818, to the University in Berlin, where he died in 1831. Hegel thus spent much of his life and work in southern Germany. Clearly, although he himself did not meet Kaspar Hauser, he seems to have been woven into the circle of destiny around the princely foundling.

Hegel published *Die objektive Logik* (Objective Logic), the first part of his great *Wissenschaft der Logik* (Science of Logic) in 1812, the year of Kaspar Hauser's birth. During the remaining years in Nuremberg he wrote *Die subjektive Logik* (Subjective Logic), which was published in 1816, the year when he moved to Heidelberg. As a teacher,

he encouraged his pupils to question and even to interrupt him, and often spent the whole hour of instruction in meeting the difficulties which they suggested. It requires, as someone has said, a great mastery over a science to teach its rudiments well; and Hegel afterwards recognized that the effort to express himself with the necessary simplicity and definiteness, to free his ideas from all obscurities of subjective association, and so to bring them into relation with untrained minds, was of great service to himself, both in increasing his effectiveness as a speaker, and in enabling him to give a more strictly scientific expression to his system than it had already received in the 'Phenomenology.' [93]

Early on and throughout his life, Hegel recorded and committed to memory everything he read – and he read profusely! He had a profound respect for Goethe and modestly regarded himself as inferior to his brilliant contemporaries Schelling and Hölderlin. He celebrated Bastille Day throughout his life. Hegel was part of the group of remarkable individualities, most of them active in the arts and philosophy, that incarnated into the German-speaking world in the 18th century; the 1770's and 1780's were particularly remarkable decades:

1720's:	Kant 1724-1804
	Klopstock 1724-1803
	Lessing 1729-1781
1730's:	Haydn 1732-1809
1740's:	Herder 1744-1803
	Goethe 1749-1832
1750's:	Adam Mueller 1753-1812
	Scharnhorst 1755-1813
	Mozart 1756-1791
	Schiller 1759-1805
1760's:	Gneisenau 1760-1831
	Fichte 1762-1814
	August von Schlegel 1767-1845
	Schleiermacher 1768-1834
	Humboldt 1769-1859
1770's:	Beethoven 1770-1827
	Hegel 1770-1831

Hölderlin 1770-1843
Novalis 1772-1801
Friedrich von Schlegel 1772-1829
Tieck 1773-1853
Caspar David Friedrich 1774-1840
Schelling 1775-1854
E.T.A. Hoffmann 1776-1822
Von Kleist 1777-1811
Clemens Brentano 1778-1842
1780's: Von Clausewitz 1780-1831
Von Arnim 1781-1831
Eichhorn 1781-1854
Schinkel 1781-1841
Bettina von Arnim 1785-1859
Jakob Grimm 1785-1863
Wilhelm Grimm 1786-1859
Von Weber 1786-1826
Karl von Baden 1786-1818 (Kaspar's father)
Uhland 1787-1862
Schopenhauer 1788-1860
Stephanie de Beauharnais 1789-1860 (Kaspar's mother)
1790's: Schubert 1797-1828
Heine 1797-1856

Among Hegel's friends at the Tübinger Stift (1788-1793), a theological seminary affiliated with the University of Tübingen, were:

the rising star of philosophy Friedrich Wilhelm Joseph Schelling (1775-1854) and the aspiring poet Friedrich Hölderlin (1770-1843). Hegel's early work is influenced by Schelling and the philosophy of nature that later secured the younger man's fame, but Hegel spent years trying to emancipate himself from his friend, and their relationship suffered accordingly. Hölderlin's thought, particularly his endorsement of the hen kai pan *(Greek: one-in-all), also occupied Hegel long after he parted ways with the poet, who suffered from mental illness from 1806 until his death in 1843.* At the Stift, however, the three friends were inseparable, [emphasis – TMB] *consumed with the desire to complete Kant's philosophical project, which was the charge of German philosophy of that generation. In a nutshell, this involved recalibrating the relationship between the subject and object of knowledge, understanding the role of ethics, nature, religion, art and the state in modern life. The French Revolution was the most influential historical event for the young Hegel:* he and his friends enthusiastically followed the events in France in hopes that a 'philosophical' revolution would ensue in the German states through the agency of the mind, without violence and bloodshed [emphasis – TMB].[94]

Around 1800 the age of Gabriel (1510-1879) was nearing its peak. Its hallmark – as always in every Gabriel age – was to enable mankind to incarnate more fully into the physical world. The British had taken a leading role in this, aided by the remarkable development of natural science that had taken place in Britain since 1600 and the integration into British life of the ideas of Francis Bacon and his Arabian-inspired thinking, or 'Moon science.' This phase of materialist thought in human development would peak in the 1840's; the preparation for the succeeding Age of Michael (1879-2233) would then begin in earnest when 'the War in Heaven' began in the spiritual sphere nearest the Earth – the Moon sphere – and Michael and his hosts ejected the ahrimanic angels out of the Moon sphere down into the human realm. The end of the 18th and the beginning of the 19th centuries thus saw the Michaelic forces planting the human seeds on Earth that would then ripen in the course of the 19th century, looking forward to the beginning of Michael's regency in 1879. This new Sun phase ('Sun science,' or spiritual science) would be led by the German-speaking peoples.

While the English were pushing ahead an empirical doctrine of evolution through accidental natural causes, the Germans were developing, through the primary inspiration of Hegel, an 'idealist' doctrine of evolution through the will of some great transcendent will (the world Spirit) ...seeing all history, all human events as 'guided' by this powerful spirit. This task of learning or of science was to Hegel (and the Hegelians after him) therefore not just to collect facts, but to discern the particular movement of this guiding hand in the midst of such facts.[95]

In his *Phänomenologie des Geistes* [Phenomenology of Spirit, sometimes translated as The Phenomenology of Mind], written in 1807, Hegel wrote: "A new epoch has arisen. It seems as if the world-spirit had now succeeded in freeing itself from all foreign objective existence, and finally apprehending itself as absolute mind."

Knowledge of the sense-world (achieved through modern science) around man is only a starting point for Hegel in the development of human consciousness. Higher than such knowledge is the kind of consciousness that connects the human spirit with the transcending Absolute Spirit. Scientific or rational knowledge acts analytically – to separate the objects of knowledge into discreet categories. It also separates, even isolates, the human Geist (mind or spirit) from the reality around it. While such reason is useful to human life, it is not itself the highest or ultimate attainment of the human spirit. That comes in a process of unification – not separation – of the human consciousness with the reality around it. Along the way in the process the human mind passes through several stages of development: from mere consciousness to a maturer self-consciousness, to the realm of reason, but then also to the stage of connection with the larger realm of reality through revealed religion and its formal declarations, to finally a virtually mystical bond with Absolute Reality. Here the human mind comes to know itself as pure spirit – in its union with the pure spirit of the Absolute. This is what Christianity, as presented by Jesus, is ultimately all about.[96]

The analytical stream of thinking devoted to the material world that was represented mainly by British culture, and had been developing since Francis Bacon, was being complemented around 1800 by the more synthetic stream dedicated to seeing the spiritual in everything. This stream had its focus in German-speaking culture, in Hegel and the other German idealists and cultural figures.

In great historical developments such as these, streams that ought to complement each other can – through mutual incomprehension or malevolent actions – sometimes conflict. By 1800 the English way of seeing things in science, politics, philosophy and the arts had been all the rage in Europe for a hundred years. It would not be easy for any other perspective to establish itself.

> *Hegel's point of view was essentially opposed to the current views of science. To metamorphosis he only allowed a logical value, as explaining the natural classification; the only real, existent metamorphosis he saw in the development of the individual from its embryonic stage. Still more distinctly did he contravene the general tendency of scientific explanation. "It is held the triumph of science to recognize in the general process of the earth the same categories as are exhibited in the processes of isolated bodies. This is, however, an application of categories from a field where the conditions are finite to a sphere in which the circumstances are infinite." In astronomy he depreciates the merits of Newton and elevates Kepler, accusing Newton particularly, à propos of the distinction of centrifugal and centripetal forces, of leading to a confusion between what is mathematically to be distinguished and what is physically separate. The principles which explain the fall of an apple will not do for the planets. As to colour, he follows Goethe, and uses strong language against Newton's theory, for the barbarism of the conception that light is a compound, the incorrectness of his observations, etc. In chemistry, again, he objects to the way in which all the chemical elements are treated as on the same level. (Encyclopedia Britannica 'Hegel' article, 1911).[97]*

In the developing confrontation that would begin in earnest in the 1840's between the Sun Archangel Michael and the ahrimanic angels in the Moon sphere, Hegel achieved something in his *Science of Logic,* mostly written in his Nuremberg years, that Rudolf Steiner described as wresting the ahrimanic thinking of logic from Ahriman's clutches. Steiner put it thus:

Anyone who understands Hegel, and the way he has developed his 'Logic,' can see how humanity in his time was starting to calcify, to become materialistic... That time was like sinking into matter in the realm of knowledge, in the process of cognition. And there appears to one, as in a picture, this humanity sinking into matter, and Hegel as it were standing in the middle, working out with the greatest energy and wresting from Ahriman the good that he possesses: abstract logic – which we need for our inner liberation, and without which we cannot ascend to pure thinking – wresting it from the earthly powers and presenting it in its full cold abstractness so that it should not live in that element in the human being which is Ahrimanic, but should ascend into human thinking. Yes, this Hegelian Logic has been snatched away, wrested from the Ahrimanic powers and given to humanity. It is that which humanity needs, and without which we cannot progress further... Thus Hegel's Logic is actually something eternal, and thus it must work on. It must be sought again and again. One cannot manage without it.[98]

Clearly, Steiner saw in Hegel's *Science of Logic* something of world-historic importance, something that was vital to any serious spiritual scientific endeavour. In Hegel's work, especially in his *Science of Logic*, as Michael's heavenly Cosmic Cultus brings to an end his centuries-long cosmic school, one can see a truly Michaelic deed, which prefigures Steiner's own *Philosophy of Spiritual Activity* (1894), written at the opening of the Michael Age itself; in both works the two men got right inside the belly of the beast, so to speak, dealing with the abstract spirit of the age on its own terms.

There is... a spiritual force in this Hegelianism, and in it there is something that must be taken up by every spiritual world view. For any spiritual science would succumb to 'softening of the bones' if it could not be permeated by that bony idea-system which was wrested by Hegel from the scleroticising Ahriman. One needs this system. One must, in a certain way, grow inwardly strong by means of it. One needs its cool mindfulness if one is not, in spiritual striving, to drift fatally into warm and nebulous mysticism.[99]

The idealism and the tendencies towards mysticism that lie within the German soul would not be able to deal with the calculating, quantitative world-manipulating approach valued in British culture if they were not stiffened with an antidote from the Ahrimanic realm itself. The interpenetration of these two very different elements, which ought to be complementary, would lay the basis for the confrontation between the two cultural worldviews that emerged in the mid-19th century and would culminate in the disaster of the First World War, during which Rudolf Steiner said:

...a saying formulated by Hegel and the Hegelians: 'The self-consciousness of thought' is meaningful only in German. Something that is an abstraction for non-Germans is, for a German, the greatest experience it is possible to have, if he understands it in a living sense. The German language sets out to found a marriage between what is of itself spiritual and what is spiritual in the thought.[100]

And about the British, he said that in them

...lies the greatest talent for purely logical, that is unspiritual thinking, as well as for systemising everything. Nothing could be a better expression of this organisational talent than the writings of Herbert Spencer. In regard to everything scientific the English people have the organisational talent. That is why they have such a flair for instituting systems for everything all over the world.[101]

The origin of these differences lay in the two cultures' different approaches to the spirit, as exemplified in the writings of Steiner himself and those of Sir Oliver Lodge.

There is indeed a kind of opposition between two things that came into being more or less simultaneously when, on the one hand, Sir Oliver Lodge pointed to the spiritual world in a materialistic way

(Lodge's book: Raymond; or, Life and Death. With examples of the evidence for survival of memory and affection after death, *London, 1916), while at the same time I was writing my book* Vom Menschenrätsel *(The Riddle of Man GA 20)... There is no greater contrast than that between the book by Oliver Lodge and the book* Vom Menschenrätsel. *They are absolute opposites; it is impossible to conceive of any greater contrast.*[102]

But Steiner went further: within the world-historical contest that was about to develop after the defeat of Napoleon between the English and German-speaking worldviews a secret was concealed – a secret that was known in the occult circles of Britain but not in those of Central Europe until the time of Steiner himself. He expressed it in this way:

If you become familiar with the most deeply esoteric teachings of the secret societies of the Anglo-American peoples, you can actually, from the point of view of content, scarcely find anything other than Hegelian philosophy. But there is a difference, which lies not in the content, but in the way it is treated. It lies in the fact that Hegel looks upon the whole thing as something quite open, while the secret societies of the West are careful to ensure that what Hegel presented to the world does not become generally known – that it remains an esoteric secret doctrine. What is the actual reason for this?... The reason is, that if one regards any content of this kind, which is born out of the spirit, as a secret possession, it gives one power, whereas if it is popularised it no longer gives this power... This is no less than a universal law – that something, when popularised simply brings knowledge, brings power when it is kept secret.[103]

Steiner was here pointing to something that would be of the greatest historical significance in the 19th and 20th centuries – the knowledge and application of the Hegelian principle of the dialectic in social and political affairs by western occult circles and also the concomitant defamation of Hegel in western society by those same circles: using Hegel for their own ends on the one hand, while on the other, ensuring that his name and his ideas would either be ignored or decried by the western public. There have been clear examples of this in recent years in, for example, the publication of Francis Fukuyama's infamous and influential book *The End of History and the Last Man* (1990) with its abuse of Hegel at the hands of his Franco-Russian misinterpreter, Alexandre Kojève. Fukuyama of course stands within the American neo-conservative policymaking nexus that has had such influence in the last decade, not least in the Iraq invasion project fomented by the group of which he is a member – the Project for New American Century. Three generations of the males of the Bush family – George H.W. Bush, his father Prescott Bush and his son George W. Bush have been members of the secret society, Skull and Bones, which was founded at Yale University in the last year of Kaspar Hauser's life by students who had allegedly established it as a chapter of a German crypto-masonic secret society. The British scholar Anthony C. Sutton (formerly of Stanford University) has rendered a signal service in exposing the activities, influence and philosophical underpinnings of this group in his book *America's Secret Establishment – An Introduction to the Order of Skull and Bones,*[104] and has shown how the group bases its modus operandi on Hegelian dialectic. Unfortunately, Sutton has no insight into what Hegel was really trying to achieve. Affected by his opposition to the power groups he seeks to criticise, Sutton misconceives Hegel to be the spiritual progenitor of totalitarian thought, the father of fascism. This notion has spread through western anti-establishment circles, who thus learn to loathe Hegel.

There may seem to be a huge gulf between the abstract idealist philosophy of Hegel and the pure heart of Kaspar Hauser as he appeared in Nuremberg in 1828, three years before Hegel's death, but if we consider both of them in relation to the Grail stream and Parsifal then the paradox is not difficult to resolve. Rudolf Steiner associates both Kaspar Hauser and Mani with the origins of the Rosicrucian movement. We recall that he said to Ludwig Polzer-Hoditz on 3rd March 1925 that Kaspar Hauser "worked into the Rosicrucian connection from the beginning [and had an] ...important esoteric mission for Christianity." Furthermore, he indicated not only that the seeds of the Rosicrucian movement were sown by the great 4th century conference called by Mani in the Black Sea region, but also that Christian Rosenkreutz himself received an initiation by the Mani individuality in 1459: "Within this whole stream, the initiation of Mani, who also initiated Christian Rosenkreutz in 1459, is considered to be of a 'higher degree;' it consists of the true understanding of the nature of evil." [105]

One of the few possessions that was clearly dear to Rudolf Steiner, who was by no means an acquisitive person, was a bust of Hegel, which he had been given as a young man when living in Weimar by the actor Neuffer, to one of whose children Rudolf Steiner was godfather. [106] He said of this bust that it was

...one of the few things that later accompanied me to many different places. I always liked to look again and again at this head of Hegel (by Wassmann, in the year 1826) when I was deeply immersed in the world of Hegel's ideas. And this, as a matter of fact, happened very often. This countenance, whose features are the most human expression of the purest thought, constitutes a life-companion wielding a manifold influence.

Let us look again at what Rudolf Steiner had to say about Hegel in order to shed some light on the spiritual impulse that lay within him and that descended with him and so many of his generation to prepare the Central European spiritual space for Kaspar Hauser:

This inwardly powerful element of a thought life that wants to overcome itself within itself in order to lift itself into a realm where it is no longer living in itself but where the infinite thought, the eternal idea, is living in it: that is the essential element in Hegel's seeking. [107]

A more succinct description of the essence of German spiritual striving it would be hard to find.

...trust in the carrying power of thinking. Every page in Hegel's works strengthens this trust which finally culminates in the conviction: when the human being fully understands what he has in his thinking, then he also knows he can attain entry into a supersensible spiritual world. Through Hegel, German idealism has achieved the highest

affirmation of the supersensible nature of thinking.[108]

According to Hegel, nature is nothing other than the content of the I that has been spread out in space and time. Nature is this ideal content in a different state... the human spirit discovers that the highest world content is his own content.[109]

But Steiner shows how Hegel, who expended all his energy on trying to illuminate the importance of thinking, was not himself able to pass through his thinking beyond into a supersensible world; he was destined, as it were, to play the role of a German philosophical Moses who would not himself cross over into the Promised Land.

In Hegel I perceived the greatest thinker of the new age. But he was just that – only a thinker. To him the world of spirit was in thinking. Even while I admired immeasurably the way in which he gave form to all his thinking, yet I perceived that he had no feeling for the world of spirit which I beheld and which is revealed behind thinking only when thinking is empowered to become an experience whose body, in a certain measure, is thought, and which takes up into itself as soul the Spirit of the world. Since in Hegelianism everything spiritual has become thought, Hegel represented to me the person who brought the ultimate twilight of the ancient spiritual light into a period in which the spirit became hidden in darkness from human knowledge.[110]

Hegel, who had been born 42 years before Kaspar, died in Berlin during a major epidemic of Asian cholera on 14th November 1831; that was the year Lord Stanhope entered Kaspar Hauser's life and on the 29th of the same month Stanhope took Kaspar out of the care of Hegel's brother-in-law, Baron Tucher, in Nuremberg, and away to Ansbach where on 10th December he was placed in the house and under the instruction of the tyrannical teacher Meyer. The ten years after Hegel's death were the years of the triumph of 'Hegelianism' in Germany. The subsequent expurgation and defeat of Hegelianism began in 1841 when, by a terrible irony, Ludwig von Feuerbach, son of Kaspar's protector and champion, the late Anselm von Feuerbach, gave a series of famous lectures criticising Hegel and published his book *The Essence of Christianity*. Friedrich Engels later commented on Feuerbach's assault:

> *...with one blow it pulverised the contradiction, in that without circumlocutions it placed materialism on the throne again. Nature exists independently of all philosophy... the spell was broken; the 'system' was exploded and cast aside... one must have experienced the liberating effect of this book to get an idea of it. Enthusiasm was general. We all became at once Feuerbachians.*[111]

Almost simultaneously, after the dismissal of the Prussian Culture Minister in 1841 and his replacement with Friedrich Schelling, the friend of Hegel's youth, who was appointed precisely to root out Hegelian thought from the universities, up sprang the new ideas of Materialism (Feuerbach) Existentialism (Kierkegaard), Voluntarism (Schopenhauer), Anarchism (Bakunin), and Positivism (Mill and Comte) like so many dragon's teeth!

Feuerbach's attacks were joined by those of Engels himself. In the same year Schelling also attacked Hegel with his *Philosophy of Revelation from the Right,* and in 1844 Kierkegaard's *Concept of Dread* was also directed against Hegel. Karl Marx famously inverted and perverted Hegal's dialectic in his own work of the 1840s, the decade in which the War in Heaven broke out.

> *In the period prior to 1841, European civilisation was working out social-historical problems in a domain of thinking which had been separated out from the whole, concrete life of society, the Theory of Knowledge, an abstraction made possible by the highly developed division of labour, and in particular the exploitation of wage labour. ...**December 1841 marks a discontinuity of spectacular sharpness in German philosophy** [emphasis – TMB] Just as in Einstein's physics there can be no simultaneity of events separated in space, so also, in the broader European scene, the rupture of 1841 is manifested in an array of changes, reflecting a common underlying process of transformation, which in turn has its social spectacle in the Revolutions of 1848.*[112]

By the time the Age of Michael began in 1879, Hegel, who had seen and celebrated the end of the old Thousand Year Reich of the Holy Roman Empire in 1806, was all but forgotten in the brash, strutting, new Prussian-dominated Reich that had been created in the Hall of Mirrors at Versailles in 1871.

Nevertheless, one key aspect of materialist criticism of Hegel had been correct – he had been too much concerned only with Mind and Idea and not enough with the world of the senses; he had not been able sufficiently to bridge the two for many people, and this is why the increasingly materialistically oriented philosophical bent of the 19th century was bound to reject him, whereas we today can reappraise him. There is a mystical, even Asiatic element in Hegel, namely, that he is primarily concerned with what Man has in his own soul, in his thinking, and he affirms that what Man has there is the entire cosmos. He shows a way for western Man, who had become alienated from life through his reason, to overcome his alienation through reason itself. As Steiner puts it, the greatness of Hegel is that:

> *...what comes to expression through Hegel as one of the strengths of German idealism in world views...[it] is the trust in the carrying power of thinking. Every page in Hegel's works strengthens this trust which finally culminates in the conviction: When the human being finally understands what he has in his thinking, then he also knows that he can gain entry into a supersensible spiritual world. Through Hegel, German idealism has accomplished the affirmation of the supersensible nature of thinking.* [113]

And on the question of Hegel's 'mysticism,' his recasting of ancient Asiatic wisdom, Steiner wrote:

> *... in the third volume of his* Vorlesungen über die Geschichte der Philosophie, *[Lectures on the History of Philosophy], one comes upon the words: "Such stuff, one says, are the abstractions we behold when we let the philosophers dispute and quarrel in our study, and decide matters in this way or in that; these are abstractions made up of mere words. – No! No! They are acts of the universal spirit, and*

therefore of fate. In this the philosophers are closer to the master than those who feed upon the crumbs of the spirit; they read or write the cabinet orders in the original: it is their function to take part in writing them. The philosophers are the mystics who were present at the act in the innermost sanctuary and who participated in it." When Hegel said this he experienced one of the moments described above. He spoke these sentences when he had reached the end of Greek philosophy in the course of his analysis. And through them he has shown that the meaning of Neo-platonist wisdom, of which he speaks at this point, was at one time illuminated for him as by a stroke of lightning. At the moment of this illumination he had become intimate with such spirits as Plotinus and Proclus. And we become intimate with him as we read his words.[114]

Something of a deep cosmic inwardness, from a past mystic consciousness, reaching back beyond Jacob Boehme, whom Hegel venerated, beyond the mediaeval mystics, beyond the Neo-Platonists, back to far distant Asia, and almost indeed to Atlantis itself, reappears in Hegel in the form of an early 19th century European thinker's concern for astract thoughts. Hegel too can be said to be a kind of 'straggler from Atlantis' – of a philosophical kind!

This is related to the fact that in the lectures he gave on the European Folk Souls in 1910 Steiner said that

The philosophies of Central Europe... represented by Fichte, Schelling and Hegel ...are apparently far removed from the sphere of mythology but they are nevertheless nothing but the result of the most penetrating old clairvoyance acquired by man when he worked in cooperation with the divine spiritual beings... Hegel's world of ideas is the final most sublimated expression of the Spiritual Soul and contains in pure concepts that which the Northman still saw as sensible-supersensible, divine spiritual powers in connection with the 'I'... this philosophy... discovers in the external world the contents of the Spiritual Soul itself and looks upon Nature merely as the other side of idea. Take this on-working impulse, and in it you have the mission of the Northern, Germanic peoples in Central Europe. [115]

It is also related to why, in his wonderful book *The Riddle of Man*,[116] Steiner includes a poem by Robert Hamerling, *German Migration*, written in 1864, which describes the migrations of the ancient Teutonic peoples from Asia to Europe. He quotes from the poem the part where Teut the youth, resting with his people in the Caucasus, muses on his people's destiny, Steiner comments:

And primal mother Asia reveals to Teut his people's future: she does not only speak hymns of praise; she speaks earnestly about the people's shadow and light aspects. But she also speaks about that essential trait of the people that shows cognitive striving to be in complete unity with an upward gaze to the divine:

> *With noble features, primal mother Asia*
> *Did eye to eye to her brave son appear.*
> *"Your joy in dreams, divine inebriation,*
> *Your ancient Asian homeland's blessed warmth*
> *And heartiness will go on living in you.*
> *Of peaceful permanence.*
> *This holy ray will be like a temple fire*
> *Of mankind, free of smoke – with purest flame*
> *Will glow on in your breast and will remain*
> *Your soul nurse and the pilot at your helm!*
> *Because you love, you strive: your boldest thinking*
> *Will be the zeal to sink itself in God.*

Steiner says of Hamerling that he thinks "...of German idealism as striving – out of the being of his folk spirit, in the way demanded by a new age – toward the spiritual realities that were sought in bygone ages by the strongest soul forces of Asiatic humanity of that time." [117] This 'ancient zeal to sink itself in God,' this pure flame is what the innocent heart of Kaspar Hauser brought to the people of Nuremberg at the Candlewax Square at Whitsun in 1828 – the light of the spirit in an age of darkening materialism.

Ferdinand Lassalle and Otto von Bismarck

Seven years after the ahrimanic forces on Earth declared war on Hegelianism in 1841 and the War in Heaven broke out in the Moon sphere above, the revolutions of 1848 erupted all over Europe. In Germany, the most liberal state of Baden was at the centre of the turmoil, and eventually, King Ludwig I of Bavaria, whose functionaries had imprisoned Kaspar Hauser for 12 years at Schloss Pilsach near Nuremberg, was forced to abdicate. Without a modern Teut to lead them and unable to offer the crown of a united Germany to Grand Duke Kaspar of Baden, murdered 15 years before, the assembled parliamentarians at Frankfurt, Germany's best political and academic minds, could think of nothing but to offer the crown to the arch reactionary Friedrich Wilhelm IV of Prussia, who scornfully rejected it, disdaining to become a constitutional monarch beholden to his people.

Two very different figures, who were to dominate German political life in the 1850's and 1860's, Ferdinand Lassalle, the Jewish socialist leader, and Otto von Bismarck, the representative of the Prussian Junker class, were both deeply affected by the events of 1848-1849. The 33 year old Bismarck, already the pragmatist, recognised that, as he said, "the past is buried... no human power can bring it back to life," but he nevertheless struggled against the Frankfurt parliament, mobilising modern means of political action (press campaigns, association meetings, and parliamentary speeches) to prevent Prussia from becoming just a part of a united Germany. Ferdinand Lassalle, a young man of 23 when the Revolution broke out, was a student of Hegel and Heraclitus, whom Hegel himself had acknowledged as his forerunner. He took part in the Revolution as a member of the Communist League but developed his strongly Hegelian views in the direction of reform not violent revolution. He yearned for a moral State that could serve the people and raise them up, especially the downtrodden working class, and he was fiercely opposed to what he saw as the rapacious selfishness of the bourgeoisie and the inhuman slavery of the capitalist system. He did not therefore object to a constitutional monarchy in service to the people. For these views he was criticised and castigated by Marx and Engels, who regarded him as a Bonapartist dictator. He was still so regarded by some on the opposite wing of politics in more recent times, for example, Ludwig von Mises (1881-1973), the Austrian economist whose work has spawned the Ludwig von Mises Institute (an American neo-liberal think tank) who wrote of Lassalle in his essay: *Omnipotent Government – The Rise of Total State and Total War (1944):*

> *Lassalle's brief demagogical career is noteworthy because for the first time in Germany the ideas of socialism and etatism appeared on the political scene as opposed to liberalism and freedom. Lassalle was not himself a Nazi; but he was the most eminent forerunner of Nazism, and the first German who aimed at the Führer position. He rejected all the values of the Enlightenment and of liberal philosophy, but not as the romantic eulogists of the Middle Ages and of royal legitimism did. He negated them; but he promised at the same time to realize them in a fuller and broader sense. Liberalism, he asserted, aims at spurious freedom, but I will bring you true freedom. And true freedom means the omnipotence of government. It is not the police who are the foes of liberty but the bourgeoisie.*[118]

Both Lassalle and Bismarck were indeed opposed to the interests of the mercantile classes – Lassalle, because they oppressed the workers in inhuman ways, and Bismarck, because they threatened the interests of the landed aristocracy. Bismarck also had a canny understanding of the motives of bankers; after Abraham Lincoln's murder, he made the following observation:

> *The death of Lincoln was a disaster for Christendom. There was no man in the United States great enough to wear his boots. I fear that foreign bankers with their craftiness and torturous tricks will entirely control the exhuberant riches of America, and use it systematically to corrupt modern civilisation. They will not hesitate to plunge the whole of Christendom into wars and chaos in order that the Earth should become their inheritance.*[119]

In the last two years of Lassalle's life (he was killed in a duel over a woman on 31st August 1864) these two unlikely partners were actually drawn together. By now they both believed in a united Germany: Bismarck in one dominated by Prussia, and Lassalle in one dominated by neither Prussia nor Austria. Lassalle founded the General German Working-men's Association, the organisation, which would later become today's Social Democratic Party (SPD), on 23rd May 1863, and in the same month began a correspondence between the two men which continued until February 1864. Lassalle initiated a series of clandestine meetings with Bismarck in the winter of 1863-1864 where the two discussed mostly universal suffrage and the idea of State aid for workers' associations (later developed by Bismarck into the world's first State-run social insurance scheme). Lassalle was keen to get both these ideas realised as soon as possible, while Bismarck was more cautious. The ever self-confident Lassalle even declared during his trial for high treason at the time:

> The prosecutor accuses me of wishing to introduce universal and direct suffrage, and thus to overthrow the Constitution. Well, gentlemen, although I am but a private individual, I may say to you: not only do I wish to overthrow the Constitution, but perchance, ere one year shall have passed, I will have overthrown it! But how? Without one drop of blood having been shed, without a hand having been raised in violence! Perchance not another year shall have passed, but universal and direct suffrage will have been introduced by the Government in the most peaceful manner in the world. The strong hands, gentlemen, can be played with exposed cards! It is the strongest diplomacy that does not need to conceal its calculations with any secrecy, because it is founded upon iron necessity. And so I proclaim to you, here in this solemn spot, perchance not another year shall pass – and Herr von Bismarck will have played the role of Robert Peel, and universal and direct suffrage shall have been proclaimed! [120]

Further possibilities between the two men were terminated by Lassalle's death in the duel. One of Lassalle's strongest supporters was

Countess Sophie von Hatzfeld, who owed Lassalle a great deal as he had devoted eight years of his life to saving her honour as her legal representative in her battle against her ruthless husband. The 23-year-old Lassalle took on this task, claiming that "his sole motive had been one of pity for a persecuted woman, deserted by her friends, the victim of her social position, the object of the brutal persecution of an insolent aristocrat." [121] The Countess's reward for Lassalle's successful representation of her case was to grant him an annual income of 7,000 thalers (£1,050) which took care of his finances for the rest of his life. She also opened the doors of high society for him and facilitated his meetings with Bismarck. Of Lassalle, Bismarck said:

> *He was one of the most cultured and kindest men I have ever had dealings with, a man who was ambitious in a grand way and not at all a republican; he had an expressly national and monarchical cast of mind. The idea to which he strove was that of the German Empire and therein we had a point of contact. Whether the German Empire should be brought about by the Hohenzollern dynasty or by the Lassalle dynasty was perhaps a question, for his way of thinking was monarchical through and through.* [122]

Here is a leitmotif in Lassalle's life: although he worked for the working class and for what he conceived of as the nation, he stood in his feeling life close to aristocracy and monarchy. Born in the Romantic era three years before Kaspar Hauser's appearance in Nuremberg, Lassalle as a 15-year-old Jew, fiercely proud and idealistic, declared: "I think I am one of the best Jews in existence, although I disregard the Ceremonial Law. I could, like that Jew in Bulwer's *Leila,* risk my life to deliver the Jews from their present crushing condition [*Leila* is a novel by Sir Edward Bulwer Lytton, friend of Disraeli and Stanhope – TMB]. I would not even shrink from the scaffold could I but once more make of them a respected people. Oh! when I yield to my childish dreams, it is ever my favourite fancy to make the Jews armed and free, with myself at their head." He saw himself throughout his life as a champion of the oppressed. After seeing Schiller's *Fiesco,* he remarked:

I know not, although I now have revolutionary-democratic-republican inclinations with the best of them; yet I feel that in Count Lavagna's place I would have acted just as he did, and would not have contented myself with being Genoa's first citizen, but would rather have stretched forth my hand to the crown. From this it seems, when I look at the matter in the light of day, that I am simply an egotist. Had I been born prince or ruler I should have been an aristocrat, body and soul. But now, as I am only a poor burgher's son, I shall be a democrat in good time.[123]

After his studies of Hegel at university and his thesis on Heraclitus: *The Philosophy of Heraclitus the Dark of Ephesus*, in 1857, aged 32 he embarked on a work of historical drama à la Schiller. It was the story of the tragic knightly hero Franz von Sickingen (d.1523) and his friend Hutten who represent the struggle against the supremacy of Rome and the avarice of princes, and for the unity of the Empire, two themes which happened to be favourites amongst liberals in the 19th century. "What we desire," says Sickingen:

> *That is a single Deutschland, mighty, great,*
> *A shuttering of all government by priests,*
> *A final breaking with all Roman ways,*
> *Pure teaching that is Deutschland's only church,*
> *A new birth quite commensurate with the old,*
> *Of old Germania's common liberty;*
> *Complete destruction of our Princelings' sway*
> *And of the rule by middlemen usurped,*
> *And mighty stress and strain of time,*
> *Firm based and deeply rooted in her soul*
> *One evangelic chief as Kaiser at the head*
> *Of the great realm.*[124]

This is an image of a moral polity, a moral State, a moral community, led by one who is himself moral – an 'evangelic chief.'

* * *

Paul Marks, of the rightwing Libertarian Alliance (motto: Life, Liberty and Property) has claimed that Otto von Bismarck is to blame for the totalitarian catastrophes of the 20th century: "In 1862 Germany was well on the way to becoming a libertarian area and this would have led to a libertarian world. One man prevented this and shifted German and world history onto the path of state dominance." [125] Blaming the man of will, of 'blood and iron,' for setting Germany on its anguished twentieth century path has been common for decades and there are those, such as von Mises who would do the same for Lassalle (*"Lassalle... the most eminent forerunner of Nazism"*). But this is far too facile an analysis. Both men, Lassalle, the man of ideals, and Bismarck, the man of resolute will, had something of the true German spirit in them. They did indeed oppose the rising power of the capitalists of their day and their political representatives, but they were missing the one between them who could have united them: Kaspar Hauser. He could have been the thinking heart centre that could have related the man of feeling and imagination with the man of will and instinct – Lassalle and Bismarck. Until Stanhope's arrival, Kaspar Hauser was surrounded predominantly by middle class people in Nuremberg: only Feuerbach and von Tucher were minor aristocrats. Kaspar not only would have had a feeling for the rising middle classes if he had managed to reclaim his throne after the age of 21; he would have been the 'evangelic chief' that Lassalle sought. He had both the kingly and the shepherd nature in himself.

Prince Albert, Richard Wagner and Ludwig II of Bavaria

Seven years after the death of Kaspar Hauser, Prince Albert of Saxe-Coburg married the young Queen Victoria of Great Britain. Like the marriage of another Anglo-German royal couple more than 220 years before, that of Frederick V of the Palatinate and Princess Elizabeth, daughter of King James I (1613), this marriage promised much but was tragically cut short in its heyday by the Prince's premature death at the age of 42 in 1861. Albert was liberal, very able and conscientious with a strong sense of what a liberal monarch could achieve in the modern world;

he worked hard for understanding between Britain and the German states and achieved much in his 21 years in Britain. But there was so much more he could have done to wean Britain from its harsh and crassly materialist ways. A year after Albert died, Bismarck became Minister-President in Prussia. Had Albert lived, Bismarck would probably not have had things all his own way in foreign affairs. If Albert had been able to cooperate with a King Kaspar of a united Germany or even with a Grand Duke Kaspar of Baden, things may well have gone much better between Britain and Germany. In the year of Revolutions, 1848, Albert drew up an ambitious plan for a 'Federative State' in Germany with a strong sovereign, chancellor and parliament that would maintain 'the States complete in themselves' as well as their 'dynastic forms,' which he regarded as the embodiment of the 'Individualities of these People.' Albert trained his daughter Vicky in his own liberal views and ways (his son Bertie, later Edward VII, by contrast, was quite incapable as a child), and she later married Crown Prince Frederick of Prussia, who was like a second Albert, but rather less able. Without the advice of his father-in-law, Frederick and his wife Vicky were unable to deal with Bismarck, whose guile outflanked them at every turn. They too, however, would have been aided by a mature Grand Duke or King Kaspar. The final tragedy was that Frederick also died early – of cancer of the throat – after a reign of only 99 days in 1888. Kaspar, Albert, Frederick: three great losses for Anglo-German relations. Instead, the two countries were saddled with the worst of worlds after 1888: Kaiser Wilhelm II and his uncle Edward (Bertie), Prince of Wales (King Edward VII 1901-1910), who both loathed each other. Their mutual antipathy greatly influenced Britain's radical diplomatic realignment – the formation of the Triple Entente – during the reign of Edward VII, who played a significant part in the Entente's creation. In place by 1907, this anti-German 'alliance' between France, Russia and Britain would lead directly to catastrophe seven years later.

* * *

As with Lassalle, two more different characters could hardly be imagined than Bismarck and the dreamer King Ludwig II of Bavaria (1864-1886), the builder of castles, the so-called 'Mad King' or 'Swan King.' And yet, between these two there was also mutual respect and a certain admiration. Bismarck had a portrait of Ludwig in his study, and the two men corresponded throughout Ludwig's reign, although they only met once. Ludwig often asked Bismarck for advice, and was another tragic figure who was, as it were, waiting for, or missing Kaspar Hauser. He idolised Lohengrin and the operas of Wagner; indeed, he was the man who made Wagner possible, for without his patronage, it is likely that Wagner would not have become the success that he did. He himself was in no doubt as to the debt he owed the King. The archetypal Romantic monarch, Ludwig was crowned in 1864, the year of the Romantic politician Lassalle's death, and as almost his first act, summoned Wagner to him that same year. He said to Wagner:

> *I want to lift the menial burden of everyday life off your shoulders for ever. I want to enable you to enjoy the peace you so long for, so that you will be able to unfurl the mighty pinions of your genius unhindered and in the pure ether of your rapturous art! Unknowingly, you were the sole source of my joy from my earliest boyhood, my friend who spoke to my heart as no other could, my best mentor and teacher.* [126]

Born on the 25th August 1845, almost exactly 33 years after Kaspar Hauser, Ludwig had spent much of his life at his father's castle of Hohenschwangau; he was to build his own Neuschwanstein Castle nearby. From ancient times this southeast corner of Germany had been intimately connected with the motif of the Swan. There is Schwangau and the Swan Lake (*Schwan-See*), and the lords of Schwanstein had built their castle in the 12th century when the saga of the Swan Knights was still alive. Lohengrin had been Parsifal's son. [127] At the age of 15, Ludwig had seen a performance of Wagner's *Lohengrin* and had been profoundly moved by it, identifying himself with the Swan Knight. The image of the Swan Knight figured in Kaspar Hauser's life also; in the year of his death in 1833,

12 years before Ludwig was born, he was confirmed in the Chapel of the Order of the Swan at St Gumbertus church in Ansbach (20th May) by Pastor Fuhrmann. About the Order of the Swan, which was founded on Michaelmas day, 29th September 1440 by Friedrich II, Prince of Brandenburg, Rudolf Steiner said: "Those dedicated themselves to the Order of the Swan who wished that the Grail Knights would work through them here on the Earth. And such a man was called a Swan through whom a Grail Knight worked here in the physical world. In this connection Rudolf Steiner went on to indicate the Lohengrin Saga..." [128] These 'Swans' or Swan Knights were known as 'living dead' (lebendigen Toten) who in this world served the Grail Knights on the other side of the threshold as living 'sheaths.'

A study of Ludwig's biography shows him to have been another tragically flawed figure, hardly in this world, so much did he live in the world of his imagination that was focused on the Middle Ages. It is sometimes said that his own family had him murdered because his castle and palace-building expenses were bankrupting the dynasty (Bismarck for one suspected this), and yet, today, Ludwig's 'follies' draw millions of tourists (with their euros!) to Bavaria to gaze in wonder. What may seem at the time to be a glorious error or failure can sometimes turn out to be a resounding success. Looking at the world-famous Neuschwanstein Castle (New Swan Stone) in its glorious setting against the backdrop of the majestic Alps, with its gleaming white walls and red frontage, its courtyard wall paintings of St Michael and the Virgin Mary, its grand rooms all decorated with splendid scenes from Wagner's operas leading up to the Great Hall dedicated to the story of Parsifal, who seems himself to be the knightly statue up on the castle roof staring out towards the Alps – looking at all this and taking it in, is it only fanciful to think that Ludwig was dreaming of just that Grail Centre in southern Germany that Rudolf Steiner indicated to Ludwig Polzer-Hoditz was prepared by the great generation of German idealists to receive Kaspar Hauser?

And had not Richard Wagner tried his best to conjure up in his art the Grail mood of the mediaeval past? Had he not prepared for this with his mighty Ring Cycle, based on the story of Siegfried and the Nibelungs, an epic that in its origins reached back to the Atlantean origins of the Teutonic peoples as well as to their more recent struggles against Attila and the Huns? Was his work not paralleled in England by Tennyson's *Idylls of the King* and other Arthurian lays? Was not the mood of the Grail in many such forms seeking to break through in the period 1812-1895 that Kaspar Hauser might have lived through to old age? Could not this mood and atmosphere of spiritual idealism have been catalysed by a great individuality such as Kaspar Hauser in his role as 'priest-king' of a Central European Federation? In the West, in Britain, monarchy had had no real power or meaning since the so-called Glorious Revolution of 1688 when William III basically agreed to rule with the consent of the country's powerful Whig oligarchs; the Georgian monarchs of the 18th century had been most uninspiring. Prince Albert from Germany was a new wind and brought a new spirit. In Germany itself, the time of monarchs was not yet quite over as it was in Britain. There was still something a righteous monarch could achieve and inspire.

Chapter 6

Kaspar Hauser's Life: Its Sevenfold Rhythm and Historical Consequences

In his book *Kaspar Hauser – The Struggle for the Spirit*, Peter Tradowsky examined aspects of the 33-year rhythms that follow from Kaspar Hauser's destiny, both from his birth and from his death. In what follows, we shall imagine an unfolding tableau of Kaspara's life in periods of seven years against the background of 19th century events, on hte assumption that he would have lived to the age of about 90 and always with the thought in the background: what do these events suggest about Kaspar Hauser's spiritual origins?

Before looking at Kaspar's life in seven year periods, however, let us consider three specific years when Kaspar, if he had lived to old age, would have been 72, 84 and 90 respectively.

1812 + 72 = 1884
In this year Anton Bruckner began composition of his mighty 8th Symphony (completed 1887), the Scherzo which he referred to as his 'German Michel.' 'Der deutsche Michel' is a representation of the German folk soul that goes back to mediaeval times, and the 8th symphony as a whole certainly has a wondrous Michaelic and Sun-like quality. The symphony was dedicated to the hapless Habsburg Emperor Franz Josef (reigned 1848-1916) who missed the opening performance as he was out on a hunting trip! In 72 years the Sun moves through one degree of the zodiac; one can feel that the symphony was dedicated to the wrong monarch.

1812 + 84 = 1896

Uranus orbits the Sun once every 84 years (7 x 12). In esotericism 7 is the number of time and 12 that of space. Discovered in 1781 (Stanhope's birth year), it was the first planet known to Europeans beyond the traditional boundary of time and space, Saturn. In 1896 Bismarck had been forced to resign six years earlier by Wilhelm II and was in retirement (he died in 1898); Rudolf Steiner's *Philosophie der Freiheit* had been published in 1894.

1812 + 90 = 1902

If Kaspar had lived to the ripe old age of 90, he would have been alive when Rudolf Steiner stepped forward as a teacher of western esotericism in 1902. He would indeed have bridged the period from the era of the Cosmic Cultus of Michael which closed Michael's heavenly School and the arrival of its earthly manifestation in Rudolf Steiner's spiritual impulse – Anthroposophy, although it is possible to imagine that if Kaspar had been alive through the 19th century, Rudolf Steiner would not have had to bring Anthroposophy, as that would have been done by Karl Julius Schröer and Friedrich Nietzsche. Steiner could have concentrated on what he indicated was his actual mission – the teaching of karma and reincarnation.

1812 Moon

In this year, when the Great Comet was still visible in the sky and Napoleon attempted his ill-fated invasion of Russia, began the Moon period of Kaspar's biography, the time of the development of his etheric body. Already separated from his mother less than a month after his birth, in the middle of this Moon period, aged about 3½, he was placed in solitary confinement at Schloss Pilsach near Nuremberg and, harnessed to his cell wall, prevented from either standing or moving.

1819 Mercury

Kaspar was to spend the whole of the seven year period of the development of his astral body in his cell at Pilsach. In this year 1819, a bad year for freedom throughout Europe (cf 'Peterloo Massacre' in Britain the same year) Metternich enforced the infamous Carlsbad Decrees which clamped down on freedom of expression throughout continental Europe.

1826 Venus

At the beginning of this period still in his cell, Kaspar was released on Whit Monday, 26th May 1828, aged 15.

1831 (March) Ist Moon node

The year of destiny for Kaspar. At this time Kaspar, now 18½, was living under the care of Baron von Tucher. A year earlier, the last of the Zähringer line, Grand Duke Ludwig, had died (30th March 1830 at 3.45 am) and was succeeded by Leopold, eldest son of the Countess Hochberg, who had organised the dynastic crime in 1812, precisely to ensure the eventual succession of her own offspring. This would have been the point at which Kaspar himself should have become the Grand Duke. His own father had died in 1818 (most likely poisoned by the Hochbergs) when Kaspar was only six. Kaspar's uncle Ludwig then became Grand Duke, but had no children. On 26th May 1831, exactly three years to the day after Kaspar's appearance in Nuremberg, Stanhope arrived in Nuremberg and for the first time insisted on seeing Kaspar. He began his attempt to win Kaspar's favour, which ended in his being appointed Kaspar's guardian in December of the same year. N.B. Hegel died the month before, 14th November 1831. Goethe died on 22nd March 1832.

1833 Sun

Georg Friedrich Daumer became 33 in this year. Kaspar, aged 20, now living in Ansbach with the oppressive teacher Meyer, who was in the pay of Stanhope, was confirmed on 20th May in the Swan Knights' chapel of St Gumbertus by Pastor Fuhrmann – a profound experience not only for Kaspar himself but for all those many present who were watching. This was a few days before the death of his champion Anselm von Feuerbach,

> *During the singing Hauser knelt on a prayer stool before the altar. The moment, however, when he knelt, the emotion with which he spoke... in the silence had an unusual effect on the whole congregation. Every lip moved quietly in response; all hearts prayed with him and for him.* [129]

By his confirmation, Kaspar showed that he had discovered 'living, active Christianity' through Pastor Fuhrmann, who was convinced of Kaspar's 'emotion and exaltation of soul for our Saviour' and that 'the gospel of Christ which beatifies all believers had struck deep roots in his heart.' [130] On 29th September Kaspar was 21 years old; he revisited his friends in Nuremberg and expressed a wish to live an independent life. On 27th November, however, his enemies in Baden altered official records so that the infant for whom he had been exchanged in 1812, Kaspar Ernst Blochmann, was made officially to die in 1833 (he had of course died in 1812); this signified their decision to strike at Kaspar and kill him, which they did on 14th December. In 1833, at the age of 20, Wagner composed his first complete opera, *Die Feen* (The Fairies). Wagner later personally gave the original manuscrpt of *Die Feen* to King Ludwig II of Bavaria, and the manuscript was later given as a gift to Adolf Hitler, who became Chancellor of Germany in 1933. It was destroyed in the flames of Hitler's Berlin bunker in 1945.

Whereas the period 1815-1830 was one of reactionary conservatism in European politics and society, the 1830's promised to herald the dawn of reform, beginning with the July Revolution of 1830 in Paris (in the 42nd year after the Revolution of 1789). The Polish uprising against the Russians followed, which drew sympathy all over Europe, especially in Germany, as did the Greek revolt against the Turks. The Poles failed in their revolt, but the Greeks, who had been fighting against the Ottomans since 1821, were rewarded with recognition as an independent country in July 1832 by the Treaty of Constantinople. The Greek and Polish examples emboldened liberals throughout Germany to protest against Metternich's repression of Central Europe. On 27th May 1832, the Hambacher Fest saw approximately 30,000 people, many of them students, gather in the Palatinate to demand a liberal, unified Germany, freedom of the press, the lifting of feudal burdens, religious tolerance and even a German republic. The movement was still not strong enough, however, and after Kaspar Hauser's murder in 1833, Metternich once more gained the upper hand through the princely puppets of the German states. In Britain, by contrast, the 1830's saw the Great Reform Bill of 1832, the abolition of slavery throughout the British Empire and the Factory Act (1833) which provided for: no child workers under 9 years old, a maximum eight hour working day for children aged 9-13, two hours schooling for children and the appointment of factory inspectors. Three years after Kaspar's death, the Chartist movement arose in Britain to campaign for the rights of the emerging but downtrodden working classes and for universal suffrage. It had an enormous effect on British political life, continuing vigorously until 1848.

1840 Sun

In 1841 the War in Heaven began between Michael and his hosts and the ahrimanic angels in the Moon sphere.[131] Kaspar, in his second Sun septennial period, that of the development of the Intellectual-Mind Soul (28-35) would have illumined this with his thinking. Prince Albert married Queen Victoria. Ludwig II of Bavaria was born in 1845. His weakness was in his thinking, which was given over to reverie and fantasies.

1847 Sun

(Third Sun septennial: Consciousness Soul development) Kaspar would have been 35. In the following year of the German Revolution, 1848, as the Grand Duke of Baden, whose people were the most prominent in the liberal revolution, he could have received from the Frankfurt all-German parliament the crown of a united Germany or of a federal German union. Instead, it was offered to the arch-reactionary Friedrich Wilhelm IV of Prussia, who spurned it and whose troops later put down the last efforts of the revolutionaries in Baden. As ruler of the new self-chosen liberal monarchy in Germany, would Kaspar not have been able to guide Germany onto a different path, in cooperation with Victoria and Albert in Britain? 100 years later, after a century of the most painful and traumatic developments, Germany was given a federal constitution by the Anglo-American victors of the Thirty Years War of the 20th century (1914-1945).

1854 Mars

The Crimean War broke out over ostensibly religious motives – the protection of the Holy places in Palestine. Once again, as in the year of Kaspar's birth, 1812, the West (Britain and France) invaded the East

(Russia) while Central Europe looked on helplessly. The West attacked the East again in the 2nd Opium War 1856-1860: Britain and France invaded China and imposed their will, opening the way for 120 years of suffering in China. Would Kaspar, beginning his own Mars period (Spirit Self period) have been able to bring peace and prevent war, providing the kind of mediation between East and West for which Central Europe is actually suited?

1861 Jupiter

Kaspar would have been 49 (7 x 7) with the onset of his Jupiter (Life Spirit) period. Thirty-three years after Kaspar's appearance in Nuremberg in 1828, Rudolf Steiner was born. In 1861 the young Crown Prince Ludwig of Bavaria saw Wagner's *Lohengrin* and *Tannhauser;* in 1864 he became king and immediately offered his patronage to Wagner, securing the composer's work. The 1860's can be seen as the decade of mankind's first 'Moon Node' if each century (3 x 33 years) is taken as a single year in the life of the New Adam, 'christened' humanity. The American Civil War (1861-1865) and the emancipation of slaves in America. Central Europe's futility: the doomed Habsburg effort to establish an empire in Mexico (1864-1867) under Maximillian, son of the Austrian Emperor. Bismarck took the helm in Prussia in 1862; Lassalle died in 1864. Under Bismarck, Prussia resolved the vexed question of the future of Germany (small, under Prussia, or large, with Austria) by defeating first Denmark (1864) and then Austria (1866) in war. The Habsburg Empire adapted to the new situation by the Imperial *Ausgleich* (Compromise) of 1867, creating the Dual Monarchy, the Austro-Hungarian Empire. These events can be seen as a German Civil War paralleling the American one. Would Kaspar in his Life Spirit period have been able to solve these problems of the etheric form of the German polity? Had he been successful in 1848, such problems might well not have arisen.

1868 Saturn

Kaspar Hauser at 56; his Saturn (Spirit-Man) period would have begun. King Ludwig II of Bavaria drew up his first plans for Neuschwanstein Castle; building started in 1869 and also at Bayreuth for a Wagnerian centre for the arts. 1870-1871 Franco-Prussian War and the founding of the Second German Empire by Bismarck under Wilhelm I of Prussia, in the Hall of Mirrors at Louis XIV's Palace of Versailles following the defeat of France. In 1869 Wagner and Nietzsche met for the first time; in 1871 Wagner composed the opera *Siegfried,* third part of the *Ring* cycle, and in 1874, *Götterdämmerung.* Lenin was born on 22nd April 1870.

1875 Uranus

Kaspar Hauser would have been 63. The War in Heaven was brought to a successful conclusion by Michael and his hosts in November 1879, by which time the ahrimanic angels had been cast out of the Moon sphere of the spiritual world into the etheric realm of the Earth and into the thoughts, and in some cases etheric bodies, of human beings. In the 1770's Christian Rosenkreutz (in his incarnation as Count St Germain) had said to the Countess d'Adhemar that he would be seen again in Paris "in three generations;" in 1875 the Theosophical Society was founded by Helena P. Blavatsky in New York. Nietzsche was becoming estranged from Wagner in this period. 1878 Congress of Berlin: Bismarck, without Kaspar Hauser, was 'defeated' by Disraeli and Salisbury, who persuaded the Congress to set up the Balkan preconditions that would provide the tinderbox for the catastrophe of the Thirty Years' War of the 20th Century 1914-1945. Leon Trotsky was born 7th November 1879, Stalin 11 months earlier 18th December 1878.

1882 Neptune

Kaspar Hauser 70: 101 years earlier, in 1781, Uranus had been discovered and Stanhope was born. In 1883 'the magician' Wagner died, and three years later was followed by Ludwig II, who had been declared insane by his own government, anxious to get rid of him as his buildings were bankrupting his family. A good swimmer, his drowning in only waist-deep water in Lake Starnberg was suspicious. In late 1888 Nietzsche began to show signs of drowning in his own madness, having first savagely turned against the dead Wagner in *The Case Against Wagner.*

1889 Pluto

Kaspar Hauser would have been 77. In January 1889 Nietzsche succumbed to mental illness from which he never recovered until his death in 1900. In April Hitler was born. Perhaps, if Kaspar Hauser had been active at this time Hitler would not have appeared or else his destiny would have been different from how it turned out.

1896

Kaspar Hauser would have been 84 years old. Young Rudolf Steiner was already a published author – *Philosophie der Freiheit* (1894). Bismarck (born 1815, the year of Kaspar's imprisonment at Schloss Beuggen) died in 1898. In 1896, Rudolf Steiner was asked by Friedrich Nietzsche's sister, Elizabeth Forster-Nietzsche, to put the Nietzsche archive in order and was introduced by her to her catatonic brother. Steiner, deeply moved, then wrote *Friedrich Nietzsche, Fighter for Freedom*. In 1897, Steiner moved to Berlin to edit the *Magazin für Literatur*. In the issue of this magazine on 28th August 1899 (28th August was Goethe's birthday), Steiner published his article 'Goethe's Secret Revelation' on the esoteric aspects of Goethe's fairy tale, *The Green Snake and the Beautiful Lily*. This led to Count and Countess Brockdorff inviting him to speak to their Theosophical circle on the subject of Nietzsche. Steiner went on to speak regularly to the members of the Theosophical Society, becoming the head of its German Section in 1902.

1903

End of Kaspar Hauser's life (?) followed by the commencement of Rudolf Steiner's public work as esoteric (Rosicrucian) teacher in 1902.

Chapter 7

Conclusion: Kaspar's Spiritual Origins

In view of all that this study has brought forward thus far in relation to the phenomena of space and time in and around Kaspar Hauser's life, a tentative answer to the question: Where did he come from? may now be presented. Rudolf Steiner indicated that:

> *The individuality that hides behind the Kaspar Hauser veil is a being which worked inspiringly into the Rosicrucian connection from the beginning, and then on 29th September 1812, incarnated as the son of Grand Duke Karl of Baden and his wife Stephanie de Beauharnais. Kaspar Hauser had an important mission of esoteric Christianity to fulfil... It is not a question of who Demetrius was, who Kaspar Hauser was, but of what was to have been achieved by them. One should occupy oneself with the question as to what was to have been brought about through them, for by such a direction of investigation we shall always gain the key to an understanding of many problems."* [132]

"...to what was to have been brought through them..." In other words, to concern oneself with Kaspar Hauser is to concern oneself with the future. Let us note here that Rudolf Steiner draws attention to when Kaspar incarnated: *Michaelmas* in the year *1812*; where: *Baden in southern Germany*; and the *importance of his mission*. To the above indications let us remind ourselves that Kaspar Hauser had been *an angelic being* and that Rudolf Steiner had been unable to discover any previous incarnation of his since *Atlantis*.

These aspects of his having an angelic nature, and of having a nature that was in some sense primeval, especially soon after his appearance, are well attested to by those around him: they noted the extraordinary *keenness of his senses, his compassion and devotion.* The jailor Hiltel swore to Kaspar's innocence "even if God himself had said the opposite." Daumer felt Kaspar was a "paradisal archetypal human being." Tucher described him as "man before the Fall." Feuerbach declared he was "a living refutation of the doctrine of original sin." The word 'religion' means literally 'binding back' or more abstractly, 're-connecting' – reconnecting to the divine, which implies a loss of connection in the first place. Those who have not lost the connection do not need religion. One is reminded of the joke about the Christian missionary who preached the Gospel to a group of 'uncivilised' islanders, gave up and sailed for home, having left behind his Bible in the hope that one day God would lead some of the islanders to read it. As his ship was sailing away, one of the tribesmen came running across the water with the Bishop's Bible, saying "Bishop, you forgot this!" Kaspar was not naturally *re-ligious;* he was naturally *'ligious.'* He was after all, a being with few or no prior incarnations.

He had an aversion to material comforts and habits, to intoxicants and meat; Daumer recorded that meat made Kaspar dull. He always cared for his toy horses before himself, feeding them first. Indeed, he had an aversion to all violence. According to Feuerbach: "His whole being and conduct revealed a child in him of scarcely two or three years in the body of a youth." [133] His memory was truly prodigious, yet he had no religion or dogma; he progressed from 'natural' atheism to a profound feeling for Christ via his education by Daumer and Fuhrmann, a process assisted by his equally prodigious will and capacity to learn, which was that of all very young children. He had a strongly defined naïve and childlike sense of right and wrong and forgiveness; he blamed no-one on his deathbed, saying "no-one has done anything to me." As Daumer said intuitively, "he died with a lie, but it was the lie of an angel." [134]

When we reflect that Kaspar Hauser's life, had he lived, would have been lived throughout the War in Heaven (1841-1879) and that his actual life was lived through that period which, according to Rudolf Steiner, was descending into the darkest period of philosophical materialism (1840's onwards), that he incarnated in the Age of Gabriel – that era (1510-1879) in which Man's connection with the physical world in all senses becomes strongest and in the 2nd septennial (1721-2029) of the 5th Post-Atlantean epoch, the whole of which is concerned with the development of Man's individualism, independence, self-reliance and conscience in relation to materialism and the encounter with the mineral plane of existence; and that as this mineral plane is itself intrinsically one of fragmentation and separation (i.e., alienation from the cosmic whole), then the major task in this 5th Post-Atlantean epoch is the *understanding of the question of evil,* we can begin to sense the Rosicrucian and Manichaean dimensions of Kaspar Hauser's mission. For this 5th Post-Atlantean epoch is the first truly Christian epoch. Unlike the 4th, all of the 5th epoch will have been permeated with the conscious knowledge of Christ, and whereas the second half of the 4th epoch was overawed or overwhelmed, so to speak, by the image of the Cross and the Crucifixion, the challenge in the 5th epoch will be to awaken to the meaning of the roses of Resurrection. This will have to happen in the most difficult possible circumstances, as the events of the 20th century, for example, have already made clear, through its wars and persecutions, the terrible destruction of innocence, of Nature, of ethnic minorities and of childhood itself, for the descent into materialism will be so strong and human consciousness will become so soporific that only the encounter with radical evil will suffice to awaken our consciences to the Good. In the deepest darkness, we shall be challenged to awaken to spiritual reality.

This is what Kaspar Hauser's destiny showed to the humanity of his era and what he still shows to us today: how his deeds manifest the strengthened Christ forces and how he collaborates with the Christ Power to redeem this evil. It is thus clear that Kaspar Hauser was and is a great companion of Mani, Christian Rosenkreutz, and Christ Himself. Kaspar Hauser did not achieve much outwardly in terms of great, widely recognised historical deeds; he became known through the evil that was done to him and through the quality of his being in response to it.

During Kaspar's lifetime we see in Napoleon an example of Luciferic evil – the attempt to move history backwards to a pharonic past based on the personal talents and genetic line of one man. The inhumanity, mechanisation, degradation and slavery of the Industrial Revolution and the ruthless new financial and commercial imperatives of those such as the Rothschilds and the East India Company are evidence of Ahrimanic evil, but the treatment of Kaspar Hauser reveals Asuric evil, the attempt not to overawe or to enslave but to annihilate the human Ego.

Just as he was imprisoned in Pilsach at the age, about three, when his Ego was connecting with his physical and etheric sheaths, so he was killed just three months after his 21st birthday when his Ego, following the three sevenfold periods of development of his physical, etheric, and astral sheaths, had taken possession of those sheaths. This is the normal course of development of any human being and as such, the fatal assault on Kaspar Hauser at that age signifies an assault on the Ego of all human beings. In his development Kaspar moved in the course of just 5 years from referring to himself as 'Kaspar' and 'we,' to 'I' and finally, after his confirmation, to 'I' in relation to Christ (I-CH), and given that, according to Pastor Fuhrmann, his feeling for the Christ was profound, then Kaspar in those 5 years had recapitulated the whole course of human history – as indeed do most modern children from birth to 21 – and then had gone beyond it into a new phase of human development in which the I lives in harmony with Christ: he had realised humanity's task of the 5th Post-Atlantean epoch. This means that it is not so much the three soul forces that are in question here – thinking, feeling, willing – but the I itself. The very phenomena of Kaspar's infancy, including the initial riddle of parentage, his lack of a definite name given by his true parents, and also the circumstances of his death, point to the relationship between the human I and the nature of evil. In Faust Part 1 Goethe referred to "that power which ever strives after evil but ever causes good." By this he meant that a boundary is set to evil; there is in human existence a factor which eludes mephistophelian cunning.

The Manichaean Path is one from darkness to light – forgiveness as the way to redeem evildoers, by bringing thinking into willing. First, things must be understood for tolerance and forgiveness to arise: reconciliation must be preceded by knowledge of truth. According to Rudolf Steiner, the Manichaean Path is concerned with "cultivating the outward form of life," by which is meant the purification of one's life with others – the social life. Anthroposophy has emerged through *German* culture, which has produced Bach and Beethoven, Faust and Hitler. The Manichean Path is a way to transform society, not just enlighten individuals. German culture is in the centre of the European cultural threefoldness, which means it has an affinity with the political realm, the realm of social rights and responsibilities. Anselm von Feuerbach's daughter-in-law Henriette Feuerbach wrote in 1884 that she wanted to lock what she knew about Kaspar Hauser in an iron chest "to be opened on 17th December 1933." Unknowingly, she thereby linked Kaspar Hauser with Adolf Hitler, who came to power in that year, and also with the event of the Second Coming, mankind's perception of the Etheric Christ, which also began at that time.

Mars and Mercury

These observations bring us towards the centre of the Mystery of Kaspar Hauser. In seeking to elucidate the meaning of Kaspar's sacrifice, Peter Tradowsky writes: "The French Revolution, with its ideals of freedom, equality and fraternity could not come to fruition... the impulse given by Count St Germain could not be followed up. It was replaced by the work of Napoleon and this could itself find no continuation." The impulse of Goethe and Schiller also did not succeed in their lifetimes. Schiller died 7 years before Kaspar's birth, writing his *Demetrius*, about a young prince who, like Kaspar, died in tragic circumstances. Rudolf Steiner also said on various occasions that the Goetheans did not succeed. On 24th January 1919 in Dornach he indicated that the middle of the 19th century was a crucial turning point i.e., the 1840's, 1850's and 1860's. Kaspar would have been 36, at the centre point of his own biography and at the beginning of his own Consciousness Soul period within his biography (35-42). Steiner said that until the mid-19th century, everything was seen in terms of personal liberty by the German idealists of the Classical and Romantic periods. After the 1848 Revolution, everything was seen in abstract social terms. The middle class were given until the 1870's (approximately 33 years, 1845-1878) to internalise and act out of the abstract social ideals of the 1840's; remaining asleep, they failed to do this. The consequence was that instead of leading the liberal ideals of the 1840's over to the emerging working class movement, the bourgeoisie recoiled in fear and clung on to the upper classes, abandoning the working class; the social movement thus fell into the hands of extremist revolutionaries. Rudolf Steiner put it like this:

> *The characteristic feature of the epoch of the Consciousness Soul is man's isolation. That he is inwardly isolated from his neighbour is the consequence of individuality, of the development of personality. But this separative tendency must have a reciprocal pole and this counterpole must consist in the cultivation of an active concern of every man for his neighbour.* [135]

What was needed in the 19th century was not to look just to the individual and his separate personality, as was the tendency in the West, especially in Britain, and not to look only to the world, as was the case in the East, in Russia (the 'objective scientific' socialism of the Marxists – western abstract philosophy *religiously* taken up by East Europeans), but rather to see Man in the world. This was the true task of Central Europe – the task of the Middle: to relate the individual to the whole. This takes us back to the early 17th century (1604-1613), the beginnings of the public Rosicrucian movement and the attempted marriage between the impulses of England and Germany, symbolised by the wedding of Frederick and Elizabeth (or Ferdinand and Miranda in Shakespeare's *Tempest,* which was performed for the wedding of Frederick and Elizabeth on Valentine's Day, 14th February 1613). This mercurial Rosicrucian 'marriage' was dashed by war – the impulse of Mars, whose era (1170-1510) was supposed to have ended a century before, and Central Europe paid the price. Russia had also been invaded from the west (Poland) and cast into seven years of chaos (1606-1613). In the first decade of the 19th century, another Rosicrucian impulse, reflecting the heavenly Cosmic Cultus of Michael, attempted to break through in German culture in the impulses of German idealism and was again frustrated by war in the Europe-wide campaigns of the martial master Napoleon. Once more Russia was invaded from the west (France). Just as the *inaction* of the English (King James I) largely determined events in the 17th century struggle, so now they were decided by the actions of the British (Pitt the Younger), who continually financed coalitions against Napoleon. Into this situation Kaspar Hauser came like a youthful spiritual comet, as Dmitri had come in 1604 and as Joan of Arc had come in 1429.

Schiller wrote of Joan of Arc: "The world indeed loves to blacken all that is radiant and drag down into the dust all that is sublime." Joan was born on 6th January. Kaspar Hauser, who was born on Michaelmas Day, 29th September, must have been conceived around 6th January (Three Kings' Day, Epiphany); 6th January to 29th September is 266 days. Rudolf Steiner spoke[136] of how the pure soul of Joan of Arc defeated the luciferic element in the culture of her time, both in the English and the French, despite the fact that the luciferic element in the English power elite killed Joan. The 100 Years' War was fought by the English to assert the primacy of the ancient dynastic principle of the King's blood and genetic inheritance. This was the basis of Edward III's claim to France. Steiner indicated in his lecture of 19th January 1915 that the danger in the modern period comes more from the Ahrimanic element. It was the ahrimanic element in the English power elite, through the well-connected Philip Henry, Lord Stanhope, Pitt's relative, that contributed to the killing of the pure soul of Kaspar Hauser. The real power of the aristocratic families that dominated Britain in Stanhope's time was no longer based on 'blue blood' but on commerce, trade, industry and purely legal entitlement to land. In 1433 and 1833, the actual killing was done by natives of the victims' countries, but the power of England's elite was behind both killings. England itself has not produced any such famous pure young soul, except perhaps for the sons of Edward IV, the murdered princes in the Tower (1483) about whom little is known (certainly their deaths had enormous consequences for English history, resulting in the succession and then overthrow of Richard III, which established the Tudor dynasty).

Conclusion: Kaspar's Spiritual Origins

France was England's first great enemy; it carried the political-military spirit of the 4th Post-Atlantean epoch; Germany has been England's great enemy in the economically driven 5th Post-Atlantean epoch. The result of the killing of Joan of Arc and the victory of France meant for England the defeat of its luciferic element – a loss of political dominion in the 15th century: the loss of France and the disastrous Wars of the Roses. The murder of Kaspar Hauser led to the rise of Bismarck's imperial Germany, and England's pyrrhic 'victory' over that Germany in 1918 meant for England the defeat of its ahrimanic element – the loss of the British Empire itself in the 20th century and the decline of England's economic power (by 1917 Britain was no longer either the world's leading manufacturing nation, its leading exporter or its creditor). The English will to power was thus defeated in both cases by an innocent soul. Joan's three years of activity began a process of English development that led away from Europe and ultimately out to the world. Kaspar Hauser's five years of activity were followed by a process of British development and Anglo-German antagonism that led ultimately to the end of the British Empire – and Britain's 'return' to Europe? Or will a hidebound British elite seek to sabotage that too?

In Britain there was until recently always a tendency to defend Stanhope and underestimate Kaspar Hauser (see for example the 1911 Encyclopedia Brittanica). Stanhope's family home of Chevening in Kent is now the official residence of British Foreign Secretaries. Having completed the imperial phase of their history that goes back to 1604, when James I's peace treaty with Spain made possible Britain's oceanic mercantile advances, a phase that arguably goes back even to Henry VIII and his separation from Rome, the British now need to develop a greater degree of ethnic self-knowledge and a new understanding of their place in the world. For they have been the world's leading initiators into the principles of separation, individuation and personality – what Steiner called 'the separative tendency.' Paradoxically, this has been effected by means of the British Empire, which would at first appear to be an integrative, uniting enterprise. In fact, it was largely created through motives of greed and acquisitiveness and secured with the application of the principle of *divide et impera.* It introduced communities and individuals to the experience of an isolating individuality.

This is the Mars tendency – divide and individuate – and that was the tendency of the Mars epoch (1170-1510), a drive to engage with physicality and the mineral, symbolised perhaps by the fact that in the last decades of the Mars epoch, Europe's knights were entirely encased in steel, resembling mediaeval robots. England had fully internalised this by the time of Henry VIII and Elizabeth I, and proceeded in the Age of Gabriel to carry this martial impulse successfully into the realm of trade and commerce, which can be described as the lower octave of the mercurial. One must be clear that without this tendency, not only would there have been no natural science but also no development of a personal lower ego which could be transformed into a higher, spiritual ego: the age of natural science perforce had to precede that of spiritual science – Gabriel had to precede Michael. Taken beyond its time and taken to the extreme, however, this tendency becomes evil, and in Rudolf Steiner's words, threatens "to flood the world with the death of culture and the sickness of culture." [137]

Britain having spread the impulse to materialism through the 18th century, the 19th century needed an antidote – which was given by a Germany intended to be the focus of a new Grail culture, and above all, by Kaspar Hauser who was to be at the centre of a higher mercurial healing power of the new Grail culture that would develop fully after the beginning of the Michael era in 1879. Kaspar's path in the 19th century, like Germany's path in the 17th and 20th centuries, was a painful one of sacrifice through terrible darkness and misdeeds. In the 12 years of 1933-1945, Germany even had to experience a most radical evil. In his lecture of 19th January 1915,[138] Rudolf Steiner makes clear how German culture and history has from the times of the wanderings of the tribes in the 4th century been one of sacrifice of the folk soul element: "The Germanic soul element was sacrificed on the altar of mankind. Later this was to be repeated, though less obviously so." Here he was referring to the way in which various germanic tribes flowed into union with what lived in different areas of Europe: Anglo-Saxons in England, Franks in France,

Visigoths in Spain, Lombards in Italy. The defeat of liberalism in the 19th century led to massive German emigration overseas, mostly to North America. This is the nature of the counterpole to the 'separative tendency' – 'the cultivation of an active concern of every man for his neighbour,' the antidote to isolation and the relation of the individual to the whole.

Whereas these German emigrants had to adapt to the lands and communities they settled in, emigration from Britain, by contrast, led to the creation of new countries which were dominated by majority English speakers that saw themselves as part of the British Empire (Canada, Australia, New Zealand, S. Africa) and which subscribed to white, Anglo-Saxon, protestant values. This was the continuation of the 'separative tendency,' and indeed, in the first decades of the 20th century, there was a powerful movement to federate the white nations of the Empire, to bind them ever more closely together.

Since no culture has developed 'the separative tendency' as extremely as that of the Third Reich, it might seem problematic, to say the least, to speak of a <u>German</u> counterpole to 'the separative tendency.' But in fact, so much of the Nazi movement was the exact inversion, like a glove turned inside out, of the German Grail culture, that Steiner said was supposed to have developed. This was so even down to Hitler's great love for Wagner and especially Parsifal. The Nazis' concern for *Volksgemeinschaft* and *Volksgenossenschaft* was a shadow image of 'the cultivation of an active concern of every man for his neighbour.' In the Middle European culture of the I, the Nazis sought to eradicate the I. In the culture in which, in the age of Kaspar Hauser, principles of three-folding had put down firm roots – at least in philosophy and the arts – the Nazis preached the ancient doctine of "Ein Volk, Ein Reich, Ein Führer." The true German soul element as it had developed over many centuries was in effect imprisoned, no longer visible and in its place, the world perceived an evil incubus, alien in spirit to the proper nature of humanity in the mid-20th century: Mephistopheles in possession of Faust.

141

Kaspar's Sacrifice for the World

But the nature of Kaspar Hauser's sacrifice goes further than just facilitating how German culture in the Michael era (1879-c.2233) can complement what was brought by Britain in the Gabriel era (1510-1879). It has to do with a sacrifice for the whole of mankind throughout the rest of the 5th Post-Atlantean epoch (until 3573). Here we are dealing with the relation of the German Folk Spirit to the Event of the Second Coming, the Return of Christ in the Etheric World, which began in 1933 and will continue throughout the rest of the 5th Post-Atlantean epoch. We have to try to fathom what is perhaps Rudolf Steiner's most profound statement about Kaspar Hauser: **"If Kaspar Hauser had not lived and died as he did, contact between the Earth and the spiritual world would have been completely severed."** For after all, as Rudolf Steiner once said to Friedrich Rittelmeyer in connection with the First World War: "Things need not have turned out as they have. But what has come to pass was, after all, inevitable."

Before attempting to elucidate this awesome statement of Rudolf Steiner's about contact between the earth and the spiritual world, let us consider his comments about the German Folk Spirit itself and then recall seven statements by Peter Tradowsky in connection to Kaspar Hauser and the German Folk Spirit. In the 1910 lectures on the *Mission of the Folk Souls in relation to Teutonic Mythology*,[139] where Steiner deals most fully with the question of Folk Souls and Folk Spirits, it is noteworthy that he says *nothing* about the German Folk Spirit *after* 1413. Until that point (i.e., the beginning of the 5th Post-Atlantean, or Consciousness Soul epoch) the Germanic peoples had different tribal or regional Folk Spirits although earlier still – several thousand years ago, most probably – all the Germanic peoples had had a single Folk Spirit. He then says that the ruling Time Spirit of the 5th Post-Atlantean epoch rose to that rank from being a Folk Spirit of one of the Germanic peoples; Steiner does not say which one, and we hear nothing more about the actual Folk Spirit of the German people themselves in that lecture course.

Then on 16th March 1915 in Berlin, 100 years after Kaspar

Hauser's incarceration, Steiner speaks at some length of the German Folk Spirit in the above-mentioned course on *The Destinies of Individuals and of Nations*.[140] Here he discusses the very pregnant point in history at which a nation's Folk Spirit, a spiritual being, unites with the Folk Soul, which is the body of feelings, the soul life, produced by the people assigned to that Folk Spirit. This union can occur at different levels of ethnic or national development, but there comes a time when the Folk Spirit unites with the Folk Soul down to the point at which the physical bodies of the human beings are affected. As time goes on the Folk Spirit engraves its will ever more deeply into a people's physicality; this signifies a strengthening of the Folk Spirit's will. This engraving of the physical body occurred for the Italians around 1530, for the French around 1600, for the English around 1650, and for the Germans around 1750. Noticeably, the middle of the 18th century was the time when the first seeds of German idealism, classicism and even Romanticism began to grow (e.g., Goethe's *Young Werther*). However, whereas for the other nationalities, the Folk Spirit remained united with the physicality of its people after its 'descent,' in the case of the Germans, around 1850, their Folk Spirit ascended again into spiritual heights while still remaining connected with them, but more tenuously than the other Folk Spirits, and less connected to the physical body. This gives the Germans less of a national, and more of a universal character, says Steiner, and accounts for why they are more difficult to understand than other peoples. They have retained more flexibility; this may also be why they have and feel more angst owing to their relative lack of binding to their Folk Spirit, compared to the English, French or Spanish, who tend to be more secure and stable in their feeling of nationality.

The reason for this German phenomenon described here by Steiner is not given by him in 1915; he simply says: "these things relate to profound realities in the spiritual world." We could imagine that this may have something to do with the fact that the Germans live in the centre of Europe, and that accordingly, there needs to be more 'flexibility' of soul life in the centre, more of a quicksilver quality, which can go in any direction and take on any impress. The British today, with the Germans of the

Second and Third Reichs in mind, might object that the Germans often seem anything but flexible or quicksilvery, but Rudolf Steiner, with a longer folk memory, often says of the Germans that just that is their nature – the ability to take on whatever comes to them from the periphery and make it their own, whether it be the Catholic church, Shakespeare, French language, style and militarism, or British technology and commercial acumen; no doubt today he would refer to Americanisation.

We may notice however, that 1750-1850 coincides with the downpouring of remarkable individualities into the German cultural realm and with their returning again to the spiritual realm; it also coincides with the preparation of that southern German 'Grail' space, and it includes the life and death of Kaspar Hauser. *Could it then be that Kaspar Hauser has something to do with the descent and re-ascent of the German Folk Spirit?*

Let us now bring to mind Tradowsky's seven statements about the German Folk Spirit and Kaspar Hauser.[141] He says that:

* Kaspar Hauser brought the Folk Spirit into connection with the people

* Kaspar Hauser was the mediator for the Folk Spirit

* [Daumer] sensed that through Kaspar Hauser the connection with the Folk Spirit could be maintained

* ... it was concealed from humanity in general that he appeared on earth as the bearer of the German Folk Spirit

* ... Kaspar was sent to them (the German people)

* ... Kaspar was the servant of the German Folk Spirit

* ... Kaspar was a spiritual being working from the supersensible world

The central one of these statements – that Kaspar Hauser appeared on earth as the bearer of the German Folk Spirit – is strangely underemphasized by Tradowsky, almost as if he felt he could not be too affirmative about it, but it seems to this writer, having looked at the phenomena of Kaspar Hauser's life, that this was indeed an enormously significant aspect, *though not yet the whole story,* of the important mission for esoteric Christianity that Steiner said Kaspar Hauser came to fulfil. On the 1st September 1914, in Berlin, Rudolf Steiner made clear that Michael <u>was</u>, but is <u>no longer</u> the German Folk Spirit, and that the German Folk Spirit (in 1914) was "another Being." We can imagine that Michael may have been the single Folk Spirit for all the Germanic peoples in the pre-Christian era, after which the different tribes received their own Folk Spirits, as mentioned above. On 19th January 1915, in Berlin, Steiner stated that Michael and the German Folk Spirit are completely in harmony with each other (*durchaus in Einklange sind*). On 18-20th May 1913, in Stuttgart, he gave his listeners to understand that Michael was replaced after his rising from archangelic rank to the ranks of the Archai in 1879, but by whom he did not stipulate. Karl Heyer believes that one can infer from what Steiner said on 20th May that he was replaced among the archangels by the angel who had been the guardian angel of Gautama Buddha, who since his own elevation to Buddhahood no longer needed a guardian angel. Rudolf Steiner does not confirm this explicitly.[142]

Is Heyer on secure ground in his surmise? It seems to this writer that he is. **The Space and Time elements of the story of Kaspar Hauser do indeed suggest that Kaspar Hauser (an angelic being) was in fact the touchstone for the incarnation of the German Folk Spirit, who is a 'young' archangel (former guardian angel of Gautama Buddha) only recently promoted.** Steiner stated on various occasions that the Buddha was related to the Being Odin or Wotan, who was himself of archangelic rank and, in fact, a member of the archai who had renounced advancement to that higher rank. Wotan/Odin, therefore, worked within the sheaths of the Gautama individuality, who nevertheless had his own spirit and, as an incarnated human being who had undergone many rein-carnations, his own guardian angel. These two Beings, Odin and Gautama, who both taught their respective peoples how to reason for themselves, albeit in different ways, belonged to the Mercury stream of Beings. The Mercury sphere is associated in esotericism with the hierarchical rank of the archangels. When Gautama achieved enlightenment, advanced to Buddahood and died, his guardian angel was freed from his task.

Rudolf Steiner delicately indicated on 20th May 1913[143] that this angel of the Buddha advanced to the rank of the archangels (Folk Spirits) and took the place of Michael as he himself rose from archangel to archai status. Karl Heyer justifiably sees this new archangel, this 'young,' even immature archangel, who may be regarded as the 'son' of Wotan/Odin in that angels are the 'Sons of Life,' [144] whereas archangels are 'Life' (Fire) themselves, as the new Folk Spirit of the German people, and Rudolf Steiner speaks of him in relation to the German and Scandinavian peoples and "fresh elemental forces;" he is the one "who belongs to us all in Northern and Central Europe... the archangel of the Germanic Scandinavian world." [145] Sergei Prokofieff, drawing on Steiner, goes further and names Gautama's angel Being as Vidar, the silent one, the son of Wotan.[146]

If that young, 'immature' German Folk Spirit was the angel of Buddha, teacher of **non-attachment,** love and compassion, it is perhaps not surprising that the descent to the level where he could affect his people physically should not be so easy to achieve, and that therefore the descent was mediated through the mercurial angel being of Kaspar Hauser. Whereas the Christ Being descended into the carefully prepared sheaths of the half-human being Jesus at the Baptism in the Jordan, the 'young' archangel of the Germanic peoples descended to the half-human, half-angelic being of Kaspar Hauser. This archangel, unlike the Christ, would not have been able to descend to someone who was completely human in spirit and who had been through many incarnations. It required a pure soul, a Being who had had no incarnations since the time of Nieflheim (Atlantis), a Being, moreover, who would be able to bear and withstand the nature of evil with which it was to be treated.

The Germans, the quicksilver people of Central Europe, have a mercurial task as Goethe divined, namely, to flow into all, like a healing homeopathic dose, spreading through cultures the spiritualization of thinking. Rosicrucianism itself was a mercurial task that emerged from Central Europe c.1604. Needless to say, this does not mean that only Germans can be Rosicrucians, but rather that a spiritual stream must begin in cultural soil suitable for its fertilisation and growth, just as Buddhism began in India, Christianity in Israel and Islam in Arabia, and all spread from their lands of origin throughout the world. The tree of Christianity grew in Israel, and the winds of the spirit carried its seeds, and one sprang up in Germany in Rosicrucianism.

With regard to Germany's dual, faustian nature: Rudolf Steiner said on 22nd June 1919, in Stuttgart: "If the German understands how to spiritualise himself then he becomes the blessing of the world; if he does not understand it, he becomes the curse of the world;" this mercurial Janus-like duality is the reason why the story of *Faust* – the *Faust* of Goethe's time – is the German story. Near the end of his book, Peter Tradowsky asks: "Does anything exist which can illuminate the nature of Kaspar Hauser as if by a light?" [147] and he answers: *Kaspar's relation to quicksilver,* quoting Daumer's observation that "Quicksilver is the metal that exerts the strongest influence on Kaspar Hauser," and also Rudolf Steiner's words about the metal:

> *When human beings become ever more spiritualised, quicksilver will also become solid. At one time gold and silver formed drops, just as water does now. The fact that mercury is still fluid is connected with the whole process of Earth evolution. It will become solid when the Messenger of the Gods, Mercury, has fulfilled his mission. In the middle of the Atlantean root race quicksilver was brought from Mercury in etheric form. Had we not had quicksilver we should not have had the Christ Principle. In the drops of quicksilver we have to see what was incorporated in the middle of the Atlantean epoch.* [148]

This enables Tradowsky to come to his final conclusion, that Kaspar Hauser brought to the darkness of a Europe whose heart was being engulfed in materialism the impulse of *love,* as it has long been known in esotericism that the occult name for the Earth is Mars-Mercury – the first half or incarnating wave of earth development (involution) being ruled by the Mars principle of condensation and densification, and the second half or excarnating wave (evolution) being ruled by Mercury. In the Mars phase the cosmos is a cosmos of the cosmic wisdom that is the deeds of the Gods. In the Mercury phase, the cosmos of wisdom will be transformed into a cosmos of love through the deeds of mankind, who has been saved and 'christened' by Christ's deed on Golgotha and transformed by his mercurial healing messengers of love. Quicksilver has in it the quality of sun and moon in its silver light and flowing lively liquidity. The Japanese alternative medicine practitioner Masaru Emoto, who has done much work into the crystallisation of water and the meaning of the resulting patterns, says in his book, *The Hidden Messages in Water*,[149] that the essence of water is 'gratitude,' because water is ego-less, and gently and passively receives whatever is given to it. With this gratitude in one's heart can come the soul quality of contentment – the Christian spirit of "Not my will but Thine be done," a Buddhist mood of non-attachment and acceptance. This spirit of the liquid quicksilver can be felt in the moving words written by Kaspar Hauser himself:

> **Contentment** is the greatest worker of miracles. It transforms water into wine, grains of sand into pearls, raindrops into balsam, poverty into wealth, the smallest into the greatest, the most common to the most noble, earth into paradise. Beautiful is the heart with all its stirrings, which remains in purest harmony with itself. Beautiful is that life where deeds agree most perfectly one with the other.

Kaspar accepted his destiny by those words at his death: "Not my will, but Thine be done..." He freely accepted necessity without resistance. For what necessity did he sacrifice himself? Peter Tradowsky, in his latest book on Kaspar Hauser, published in 1998 as a response to the infamous and now discredited genetic analysis of the claim that Kaspar Hauser was a scion of the House of Baden,[150] says that for a sacrifice, a substance must be there to be sacrificed.

The word 'tragedy,' unfortunately, seems to be losing its original meaning as the media spread the modern, rather debased, sense of a tragedy as being simply a sad loss; today, when for example a child is killed in a traffic accident, this is described as a 'tragedy.' But this is not actually a tragedy in the real sense of the word. All tragedies consist of the sacrifice of something great to achieve something higher; they involve something heroic, noble and uplifting. The tragedy is in the hopelessness of the situation, but it also tears the veil between the worlds and enables us to catch a glimpse of a higher meaning, and in this way, it is in no sense depressing, but rather, inspiring. Why did the tragedy of Kaspar Hauser have to turn out as it did? Tradowsky writes[150] that human destiny is influenced by two series of facts: either by a series of incarnations or by the circumstances of a particular incarnation. The higher the being, the wider the circumstances, e.g., Christ's Passion was for all time.

Kaspar Hauser's incarnation, he believes, was determined by the historical circumstances resulting from the events of 1604. Before we consider what resulted from Kaspar's sacrifice, let us recall the enormous historical significance of the year 1604 and the period around it (1585-1623), for while the Rosicrucian impulse had long been prepared, the period 1604-1623 can with justification be called its first real attempt at a breakthrough into human consciousness.

We owe to Rudolf Steiner the fact that our attention has been drawn to the immense importance of the events of 1604 for the future development of the earth and humanity. What occurred in that year?

* According to the legend of Christian Rosenkreutz, the initiate's tomb was opened in 1604 after an interval of 120 years since 1484. The public phase of Rosicrucianism was set to begin after this event.

* Johann Valentin Andreae wrote 'The Chymical Wedding of Christian Rosenkreutz 1459,' published 1616 (the year of the death of William Shakespeare). The year 1459 was, according to Rudolf Steiner, when the spiritual individuality who had been Mani initiated Christian Rosenkreutz.[152]

* Simon Studion's book of occultism *Naometria* (Temple Measurement) was circulated (but not published).

* Kepler observed a supernova, and saw in it the sign of a new age. The two new stars appeared in the constellations of Serpentarius and Cygnus. At the time of their appearance, Jupiter and Saturn were in conjunction in the ninth house.

* The young pretender Dmitri, who claimed to be the rightful son of the last of the dynasty of Rurik, Ivan IV (the Terrible), invaded Russia from Poland and became Czar. Evidence has emerged that this Dmitri, far from being a stooge of the Jesuits, who hoped to use him to establish Roman Catholicism in Russia, had received education from a German Protestant brotherhood in Ruthenia (in modern-day Ukraine). Janusz Ostrogski, castellan of Cracow, wrote in 1604 to the Polish king that Dmitri was hidden for several years in the (orthodox) monastery of Dernański (in today's Ukraine), and that in 1603 he went to Hoszcza in Volhynia, where there was a school of the Polish Brethren (also called 'Arians'). He participated there in religious services of the Polish Brethren (he described them as 'anabaptist'). The Jesuits calumnied Dmitri after his death as an 'Arian' heretic. The Arian theologian and preacher Walenty Szmalc (1572-1622) wrote in his diary in 1604: "1604. Hic anno filius Johannis Basilii, Ducis Moscoviae, Demetrius innotuit, qui per annos 7 delituerat in Monasteriis Ruthenicis." (i.e., for seven years (1594/95-1601/02), the son of Ivan IV was hidden in Ukrainian (Orthodox) monasteries on Polish territory). According to the Polish Brethren, his 'intimate' education was supervised by Matthias Twardochlebus (probably a pseudonym; Twar-Doch means 'creator-spirit' in Polish). It is well known that Dmitri was very well educated in spiritual matters and in strategic and military affairs. The Polish Brethren were called 'Arians' by their enemies and were closely linked to the Bohemian Brothers. They were strenuous opponents of autocracy and the centralised state. Pacifists, they refused to pay taxes or to take part in wars. They had close contacts to the esoteric underground in Central Europe, from the Paracelsians to esotericists like Johann Andreae and Michael Maier. Their schools in Eastern Europe were considered among the best in Europe. They were regarded as heretics by both Catholics and Lutherans alike. A medallion of the Polish Brethren exists, from the family Przypkowski, which was made in Nuremberg in 1580. On one side is an engraving of Jesus,

with the inscription in Hebrew: "The Lord Jesus." The reverse side has in Hebrew: "In peace, a King arose, a Christ. Truly, in grace HE WAS DRAWN FROM HUMANITY." [153]

* James I's government concluded peace with Spain after decades of war. This enabled England to settle its colonies in North America without trouble.

* James I initiated the Hampton Court Conference, which began the process that in 1611 would produce the Authorised Version of the Bible.

* The Gautama Buddha Being, sent to Mars by Christian Rosenkreutz, underwent a 'crucifixion' and began the pacification of the Mars sphere.

The year 1604 occurred in the period at the onset of the Consciousness Soul epoch, which had begun in 1413. The period of the rulership of the Mars archangel Samael (1170-1510) had resulted in a polarisation of human souls as a result of what happened to them as they passed through the spiritual Mars sphere on their way to reincarnation on Earth. The increasing violence and strife in that sphere 'threatened to tear the lower ego that looked to earth away from that which looked to the spiritual ego.' This tension had been bridgeable on Earth during the late 4th Post-Atlantean epoch (i.e., until 1413) in some communities such as the Benedictines, with their principle of *ora et labora* (work and prayer), and among the Templars, with theirs of the *vita activa* and the *vita contemplativa*. In the new Consciousness Soul age, when materialism was to be developed much more strongly, a major crisis loomed, following the Mars propensity to hardening, division and individuation. Unless action was taken in the spiritual world, mankind would be split in two with no possibility of bridging the divide.

Christian Rosenkreutz determined to bridge the gap. Mars gave Man strength for incarnation (cf. iron in the blood, in plough and sword) but its outer task was now over and threatened to become unhealthy. Tradowsky says that only through transforming Mars could this be healed and that only Buddha could take on this task. He does not explain why, but we can well imagine that this was because, as an angelic being, he was related to the Wotan/Odin archangelic individuality and had himself succeeded in spreading the Mercury impulse of Buddhism to the Mongoloid peoples of Northeast Asia (Tibet, China, Korea, Japan), who carried the Atlantean heritage strongly and whose racial characteristics had been formed by the Mars Oracle on ancient Atlantis. Buddha was now united with the Christ, and the Christ could only work in the 'I' when it was not divided or split. A sacrifice was needed to enable Mars to be pacified.

We recall that Mani had united in his Eurasian movement Christianity, Zoroastrianism and Buddhism, and in the 4th century AD had called the conference that had laid the seeds of the 13th century initiation of Christian Rosenkreutz. It was then Christian Rosenkreutz who, according to Rudolf Steiner,[154] himself called a further such spiritual conference at the end of the 16th century where he laid before those gathered there the crisis that was threatening, and also his solution – to send the Gautama Buddha Being to the Mars sphere to pacify it, so that the danger of the division of humanity might be overcome. Rudolf Steiner speaks of this as the consummation of the Buddha's sermon at Benares, approximately 2160 years earlier, where he had proclaimed the Eightfold Path – the teaching of the origin of suffering and its overcoming.

Buddha's martyrdom was to bring peace and compassion to the Beings of Mars. Tradowsky notes that this sacrifice of Buddha, a Mercury Being, is always compared by Rudolf Steiner to that of Christ. In both cases a major change resulted from a sacrifice. Both met strong resistance and hatred and only through endless love and patience was progress made. The Christ Event had signalled the transition from the Mars to the Mercury phases of Earth evolution. The condensing Mars forces strengthen the incarnating Ego in relation to the physical world, and the fluid Mercury forces enable excarnation, and release from physicality, not in the sense of a fantastical luciferic excarnation but rather by a spiritualization of the 'I' in which the 'I' comes to grasp its relation to the world.

The first open evidence of the Rosicrucian impulse of 1604 is the publication in Kassel, a year after the wedding of Elector Frederick and

Princess Elizabeth, of the Rosicrucian documents *Fama Fraternitatis* (1614) and *Confessio Fraternitatis* (1615). The latter called for a 'general reformation of the whole world.' Although this new impulse was led by Christ and reflected the new cosmic order, it was at first too weak and was met by furious opposition which resulted in the 30 Years' War (1618-1648), after which it was forced to continue 'underground' for about a century (1650-1750). Into all this Central European/German development that had taken place between 1604 and 1812, Kaspar Hauser was born. His Being, destiny and life show concretely his relationship with this Mercury stream of 1604. Incidentally, even the name 'Kaspar' testifies to it, as 'Kaspar' was the name traditionally given to the dark-skinned African among the Magi, and esotericism associates Africa (specifically, Ethiopia) with the impulses of Mercury. Africa is the heart of the world, and Europe and Africa together are the world's two 'middle' continents between Asia and America.

Three spiritual streams of 1604

Tradowsky sees three spiritual consequences resulting from the events initiated in 1604: the first is the infusion of personality with a growing spiritual consciousness; thinking activated by the I becomes an organ of perception. Rudolf Steiner's book *Knowledge of the Higher Worlds and How It is Achieved* was published exactly 300 years after 1604 and shows the modern way to realise a higher world *in* this one. Steiner's verse about iron (1923) *Sword of Michael – Meteoric Iron* shows the transformation of the Mars force that can result since Buddha's Deed of 1604:

> *Oh Man,*
> *You mould it to your service.*
> *In its material value you reveal it*
> *In many of your works.*
> *Yet it will only bring you healing*
> *When to you is revealed*
> *The power sublime of its indwelling spirit.*

Where Golgotha spiritualised Earth substance, Buddha's sacrifice of 1604 spiritualised Mars substance so that spiritualised iron can become the bearer of spiritual consciousness. This is the modern Michael sword – the awakening of the soul to the spirit, as shown so well in the five years of Kaspar Hauser's conscious life.

The second consequence of 1604 is the activity of the mercurial stream. Mercury is now working in place of Mars and can overcome power, violence and oppression. Peace, powerlessness, graciousness – these have their source in the deed of the Buddha that realises the Christ Impulse. The new and youthful can always be recognised in this: the power of the clear-minded heart becomes stronger than that of logical reason. This stream is social and political in that it makes the old politics and social arrangements superfluous by striving for compromise and unity rather than partisanship and confrontation. Here we feel the influence of Mani; it is symptomatic that he is known as an arch-heretic and his true nature unrecognised, just as Kaspar Hauser has been traduced as a fake, a fraud or a fool, and his time nature is also largely unrecognised. The political nature of this stream is the will to transform all social relationships through the impulse of the Threefold Social Order. Certainly, the number of wars has in fact decreased since 1604, though it may sometimes not seem like it, because the media constantly put them before us. Wars have, however, become much worse in their nature. Power, violence, the military and fear, the 'War on Terror' (which we are repeatedly told will be almost everlasting) and security consciousness are everywhere in evidence. These phenomena are based on the decadent powers of Mars. Just as the Christ impulse has not yet been taken up by so many, neither has the Buddha sacrifice on Mars yet penetrated sufficiently. The powers of resistance grow when fed by human souls. Wars are symbols that too many still give themselves to the decadent Mars forces. This danger has grown to the point of threatening planetary extinction. The most awful events of the 20th century point retrospectively to the need for the transforming deed of the Buddha on Mars.

The third consequence Tradowsky sees is the *healing* element that can only come from the middle element that unites opposites – the true sense of the cultural impulse of Central Europe. An example is anthroposophical curative education and help for those with special needs. This middle mediating element can also be seen in the collaboration of Goethe and Schiller. Goethe found the union of sensible and supersensible in the archetypal plant; Schiller found it in artistic play – a new liberating reality. In this new type of friendship based on a union of opposites – not sympathy or destiny – new karma is created.

Buddha's sacrifice on Mars, inextricably linked to the Rosicrucian impulse and movement, is "the cosmic birth of the Central European impulse in its threefoldness: spiritual consciousness, social transformation, spiritual union." [155] This cosmic mercurial impulse infuses the heart region of Europe. It is noteworthy here that the British historian Frances Yates, to whom much is owed in that she was the first in the English-speaking academic world to treat Rosicrucianism seriously,[156] nevertheless commits the error of trying to identify the movement with Britain and especially the Elizabethan magus Dr. John Dee. But just as the Christ Event had to take place in the geographic heart of the world – Israel, midway between China and America, so the new 'Buddha Event' had to take place in *Central* Europe, in Germany. Nuremberg was traditionally the mediaeval trade crossroads of Europe, and the city of the momentous Golden Bull of 1356. It is of the greatest significance that it was precisely in that city, in whose Candlewax Square Kaspar Hauser first appeared as a light in the darkness, and that the worst forces of evil chose to broadcast the darkness of their venom throughout Europe from the giant Nazi rallies held in the very same city. The Rosicrucian Buddha Event of 1604, with which Kaspar Hauser is so connected, orients not to blood, but to release from blood ties the human being as world citizen, because he sees himself as citizen of two worlds. This ideal lives in many bearers of the true German cultural impulse, the impulse that Goethe and Schiller championed.

Finally, we can now turn our attention to the results of Kaspar Hauser's sacrifice – the heart of the issue of what was to be achieved by it, and an answer at the deepest level possible *in this study* (though not of course in absolute terms) to Rudolf Steiner's question which was posed at the beginning: *Where did Kaspar Hauser come from?*

There was strong resistance to Buddha's Mars sacrifice. In London on 2nd May 1913,[157] Steiner said that after the Resurrection, Christ united with the angels and since then had remained with the Earth invisible to human sight. In the age of Gabriel (1510-1879), something had become necessary in the age of the Consciousness Soul, namely, the development of natural science, for reasons which have already been mentioned in this study. By 1800 materialism and agnosticism were at their greatest ever levels and such feelings were being carried over into the spiritual world at death. This led to a new Christ Mystery that unites the 19th and 20th centuries. Jesus bore the Christ on Earth; in the angelic sphere he was borne by an angel. This Christ-bearing angel suffered a loss of consciousness due to the increasing materialism carried over into the angelic sphere of the Moon by departing human souls. During the 19th century "those who crossed the threshold since the 16th century resisted or opposed Christ." The whole 19th century was affected by this. There was thus a repetition of the Mystery of Golgotha in the angelic sphere – effectively a second crucifixion of Christ. It is of great significance that Rudolf Steiner spoke of this in London.[158] It would lead, he said, to *a second Resurrection* – that of *Christ consciousness* in human souls on earth in the 20th century: the return of natural clairvoyance would make possible etheric vision of Christ in the form of an angel.

One of the very earliest published lectures in which Steiner spoke of the Etheric Reappearance of Christ was given in Karlsruhe on 25th January 1910,[159] a fact significant enough in itself given the connections of Karlsruhe to Kaspar Hauser that we have examined in this study, but at that time he did not speak about the second crucifixion, the extinction of the angel's consiousness which three years later in London, in 1913 he said actually made the Etheric Reappearance possible.

> "This onset of unconsciousness in the spiritual worlds will lead to the resurrection of the Christ-consciousness in the souls of human beings living on Earth in the 20th century... the consciousness lost by humanity will arise again for clairvoyant vision... the dying of the Christ-consciousness in the sphere of the angels in the 19th century

signifies the resurrection of the direct consciousness of Christ – that is to say, Christ's life will be felt in human souls more and more as a direct personal experience from the 20th century onward." [160]

In Karlsruhe in 1910 Steiner had spoken about the ancient state of consciousness, the level and nature of self-awareness of Atlantean man and what followed it, down to the Kali Yuga period. Then he spoke of how natural clairvoyance would return now that Kali Yuga has ended and how this would enable a growing number of people to have an experience like Paul on the road to Damascus – a vision of Christ in the Etheric world, from the year 1933 onwards. In other words, the end of Kali Yuga in 1899 would give new faculties to humanity, but it is only in 1913 that we learn that it was the sacrifice of that angelic consciousness in the 19th century that actually made it possible for humanity to perceive the Etheric Christ. Eyesight can be restored to a blind man, but unless objects are put before him he will still see nothing; it was the sacrifice in the 19th century that, as it were, enabled the spiritual percept of the Etheric Christ to come before his vision – to be 'resurrected'. In Kaspar's birthplace of Karlsruhe, then, he announces the coming fact of the Etheric Reappearance without really saying what enabled it. In London, the capital city of the people whose historical task it has been to spread the values of a materialistic material science and philosophy throughout the world, and whose representative, Lord Stanhope, was deeply involved in the crucifixion of the 19th century, Steiner describes how that crucifixion would precipitate the Etheric Reappearance.

Man thus experienced resurrection of the body in 33 AD, and resurrection of consciousness from the 20th century onwards, nineteen centuries later (1933 AD). With these indications of Rudolf Steiner's in mind, Peter Tradowsky can say that in the 12 years of his incarceration, the child Kaspar Hauser experienced "as a human-earthly representative" the extinction of the angel's consciousness. The Christ forces in Kaspar Hauser were martyred, so that in this sense can be understood Steiner's words: "next to Christian Rosenkreutz, Kaspar Hauser had the greatest understanding for the sufferings of Christ" and that "If [Kaspar Hauser] had not lived and died as he did, all contact between earth and the

heavenly world would have been severed." **The transition from the 19th century 'crucifixion' to the 20th century 'resurrection' was thus made possible by the sacrifice of Kaspar Hauser.** Obviously, this was something not just for Germany or Europe, but for the whole world.

This sacrifice meant, in effect, however, also the sacrifice of the German Folk Spirit. Here Rudolf Steiner's words of 1915, quoted above, about the sacrificial mission of the German people, come into clear focus. The countries of Western and Northern Europe, as well as Russia, had already achieved national consciousness and statehood and a defined national culture in the Age of Gabriel, as was discussed earlier. Germany's turn appeared to be at hand during the Napoleonic era, but it was not so much for the narrow-minded impulses of national pride that the best minds in Germany sought to learn from the French, but rather they were attracted by the French emphasis on the universal rights of man. This was itself a reflection of the growth of the spirit of consciousness of self and of personal liberty that had been developing in humanity since the beginning of the epoch of the Consciousness Soul in 1413. It was the essentially human element that the German idealists celebrated, and which, after the defeat of Napoleon and on until the defeat of the Revolution of 1848, they sought to affirm for Germany and Europe. This noble spirit of German idealism was sacrificed by the killing of Kaspar Hauser.

The incarceration represented the extinction of the consciousness of that angel in whom indwelt the German Folk Spirit, the archangel who was seeking to descend to the peoples of the Germanic cultural realm. One human child – in whom an angel dwelt that was at that time associated with the archangel of the German speaking peoples – and another angel – in whom the Christ dwelt – had to give up their consciousnesses. As Tradowsky puts it, the *incarceration* experiment – corresponding to the extinction of angelic consciousness – is related to the (unconscious) Christ event; the murder has to do with the dynastic crime (the obstruction of the emerging strength of the 'I' in a 21 year-old). The individuality of Kaspar Hauser had managed to win through to consciousness and by the age of 21 was becoming an ever more capable young man. If his champion Anselm von Feuerbach had not been removed from the scene six months before Kaspar's own death, it is possible that somehow, Kaspar might have regained his rightful place as Grand Duke of Baden, in which case German history would in all likelihood have taken a different course. The murder made this impossible. It was the killing of Kaspar then, rather than his incarceration, that signified the sacrifice by the Folk Spirit. His slender connection with the human-angelic individual through whom he was seeking to descend to the people in his charge was cut, thus necessitating his return to a higher level of the spiritual world. This left the German people strangely bereft of their spiritual inspiration – a bereavement that was both evident in the lives of many of the finest representatives of German and Austrian cultural life in the 19th century and also felt by them, either acutely or more subconsciously. The German people were abandoned – necessarily – by their young and 'inexperienced' Folk Spirit, not abandoned in an absolute sense, to be sure, because he would still be united with them from a more distant realm of the spiritual world, but his withdrawal left them without inspiration, and that became ever clearer in the decades after 1833.

Kaspar's incarceration at Schloss Pilsach is associated by Ludwig Polzer-Hoditz with the Jesuits, enemies of the development of the 'I.' [161] It has to be acknowledged that, to date, there is no direct proof of this, though the Jesuits had always been strong and influential in the Kingdom of Bavaria with its capital at Munich (Nuremberg, by contrast, was mostly Protestant). Ingolstadt, with its university, had also been a strong Jesuit centre. It too was in Bavaria, and it had been there in 1776 that the Jesuit-trained Adam Weishaupt started his Order of The Illuminati that was modelled on the Jesuits, and yet sought to destroy them and the whole *ancien regime*. Aware of the fact of reincarnation, the Jesuits must have known that if the child were killed, he would reincarnate rapidly, as young children apparently often do. It was his human 'I' that they therefore sought to suppress by denying him the ability to walk, to hear human speech, or to experience the full reality of the world of the senses. It is surely no accident that Rudolf Steiner spoke for the first time about the phantom of the resurrection body and about Jesuit beliefs and practices in October 1911,[162] again, precisely <u>in Karlsruhe</u> and that serious hostility towards him began at just that time. But the Jesuits' actions may already have been countered by the Christ Power of resurrection working in the relationship of Goethe and Schiller, for 33 years after their collaboration began in 1794-1795 with the publication of Goethe's fairy tale *The Green Snake and the Beautiful Lily*, Kaspar was freed at Whitsun in 1828. Evil brings about the opposite of what it intends. The name 'Child of Europe' was spontaneously given to Kaspar, in July 1828, before there was any talk of Kaspar's origin. A child was given to Old Europe – an impulse of the supersensible into the sensible. Not a child of one or two peoples but of all the peoples of Europe. As Jesus had been welcomed with almost universal joy into Jerusalem on Palm Sunday, but abandoned by the fickle and forgetful populace and crucified within five days, so was Kaspar welcomed with great interest and warmth into Nuremberg, Germany and Europe on Whit Monday, but abandoned by the fickle and forgetful population after three years and murdered after five.

As the relentless but essentially fearful individuality of Lord Stanhope approached the hopeful young Kaspar in 1831 and cast his shadow over him, so did the equally relentless and equally fearful figure of Bismarck overshadow Germany in 1862, and 33 years after Stanhope intervened so forcefully in Kaspar's life, Germany in the form of Prussia was perceived by the rest of Europe to have committed its first national 'crime,' in its war against Denmark in 1864. It may seem strange to describe as 'fearful' the man who famously is reported to have declared "We Germans fear God and no-one else," but fearful he was in truth, for he was a man, like all materialists, afraid of the spirit, and his fear drove him into the fixity of his Prussian aristocratic conservatism and his feudal subservience to the House of Hohenzollern. He described himself as simply "a Prussian officer" and wished simply to have "a loyal German servant of Wilhelm I" inscribed on his gravestone. Steiner wrote of Bismarck:

I believe there would have been a possibility for Bismarck to realise his social monarchy. This possibility would have come about if Lassalle had not lost his life to Racowitza in that frivolous duel in 1864. Bismarck could not manage with principles and ideas. They lay outside the circle of his world view. He could only deal with people who confronted him with real facts. Had Lassalle lived, he would probably have brought the workers to the point where Bismarck would have been ripe for social reform plans, so that the workers would have been able to work out a solution to the social question for Germany in unison with Bismarck. To solve the social question at the right time in Bismarck's sense, Lassalle was missing. Bismarck could not make a start with the socialist parties as they developed soon after Lassalle's death, that did not wish to be led by living men but by abstract Marxist theories. If Lassalle had been there as a power factor against him leading the workers, Bismarck could have founded the social State with the King at its head, but with party doctrines Bismarck did not know how to proceed.[163]

Other great conservatives, such as Metternich in Austria at the beginning of the century and Lord Salisbury in Britain at the end of it, shared with Bismarck a marked lack of political and social imagination, or where they exercised any at all, it was only of the gloomy, pessimistic and fearful kind. With Prussia's takeover of the Reich and a growing materialism on the English model that worshipped money, power and industry, the true German spirit, as Nieztsche saw, was 'extirpated.' But this was inevitable once Kaspar Hauser was slain, for, we have come to see, he was the angelic youth bearing the German Folk Spirit, who was himself the 'young' inexperienced archangel, the former angel of the Buddha. The capacity of the criminals, says Tradowsky, resulted not only from their own intentions but from the materialism of human souls since 1600. The whole event unfolded on both sides of the threshold in such a way as to require the sacrifice of the innocent.[163] The two sacrifices – of the angel-man Kaspar Hauser on earth and of the Christ-bearing angel in the etheric world – came together in their consequences exactly a century later in 1933, when Hitler gained power in Germany and when the Etheric Christ began to be visible around the world, which signified the Resurrection of that angel's consciousness and of human consciousness of Christ.

Kaspar Hauser thus had a greater significance for the 20th century and the future than he did for the 19th century. This explains the great hatred against Kaspar Hauser, first orchestrated by Stanhope during 1833-1836 in his campaign to besmirch Kaspar Hauser's name and then continuing on until today, for example, as seen in the spurious claims made in the genetic analysis campaign against Kaspar Hauser's memory waged by *Der Spiegel*, one of Germany's leading magazines, as recently as 1996. These claims were shown by a second independently conducted genetic test in 2002 to have been based on false evidence:

> *In November 1996 the German magazine 'Der Spiegel' reported an attempt to genetically match a blood sample from pants assumed to have been Kaspar Hauser's. This analysis was made in laboratories of the Forensic Science Service in Birmingham and in the LMU Institute of Legal Medicine in the University of Munich. Comparisons with the members of the royal family were inconclusive. It later became clear that the examined pants did not come from Kaspar Hauser but probably from the exhibition of the trousers claimed to be Kaspar Hauser's in Berlin police headquarters in 1905... In 2002, however, the Institute for Forensic Medicine of the University of Münster analyzed hair and body cells that were also alleged to belong to Kaspar Hauser, and came to a more conclusive result. From different sources six samples altogether were taken: The boy's hat and trousers along with his hair curls, partially from the private collection of the Ansbacher chief presiding judge Feuerbach. The analysis took a long time as the results in the laboratory were examined several times over for the sake of accuracy. The genetic code was the same in all six samples, and was a 95% match to that of Astrid von Medinger, a descendant of Stephanie de Beauharnais, who would have been Kaspar Hauser's mother if indeed he had been the hereditary prince of Baden. The DNA evidence would seem to argue that Kaspar Hauser was indeed a descendant of the House of Baden.*[165]

Kaspar's right to be regarded as the rightful Prince of Baden was thus upheld – even on the basis of physical DNA evidence! The *Spiegel* campaign was a further example of a hatred against the ongoing Christ Spirit, for the case of Kaspar Hauser is not merely an historical one.

Many German people, and much German cultural development in the 19th and 20th centuries, were sacrificed to make possible Kaspar Hauser's greater esoteric mission for all humanity – a second Mystery of Golgotha (the crucifixion of consciousness). Kaspar Hauser was the bridge between the death and resurrection of the consciousness of the Christ-bearing angel. In this relationship between 'the two Mysteries of Golgotha' lies the fateful destiny between the 'two peoples of the middle' – the Germans and the Jews, who, some 1800 years before, were also required to make a sacrifice of their people and their culture in order to enable a mighty spiritual event to happen amongst them that was for the sake of the whole world.

The peoples of Europe will need to be able to differentiate between what comes from the Folk Spirit and what comes from the outer power of the state. It is noteworthy that the word 'patriot' is now very much in contention in the USA, for example. What constitutes a true 'patriot?' Goethe urged Germans to forget the chimera of national unity, and Schiller differentiated between Volk and Reich. Nietzsche regarded the Reich and the German spirit as mutually exclusive. True love of country means developing insight into how the spiritual world interacts with one's land and culture; it means acting in harmony with that, which may sometimes mean accepting that one's country needs to suffer, whereas conventional patriotism all too often results in blind obedience to the State and an attitude of 'my country right or wrong.' Kaspar, as Child of Europe, was given to Central Europe just as the old German polity 'the Holy Roman Empire of the German Nation' was destroyed by Napoleon in 1806, having just created a French Empire (1804) 1000 years after Charlemagne created his Frankish-Germanic empire in 800. The destinies of the two individualities, Napoleon the man of Mars and Kaspar the man of Mercury, were clearly united. It is remarkable that Napoleon's beloved son, (born a year before Kaspar, on 20th March 1811) whom he named the 'King of Rome,' and who was given the title Duke of Reichstadt after his father's downfall, was like Kaspar, also kept in a cage, albeit a gilded one in the court at Vienna. Far from his parents, who, like Kaspar's, were French and German. Under the watchful eye of Metternich, the young Napoleon II wasted away and died of tuberculosis at the age of 21, on 22nd July 1832, the year before Kaspar's death. Rudolf Steiner could find previous incarnations for neither Kaspar nor Napoleon Bonaparte. Could that mean that Bonaparte was also a kind of angel being – a retrograde one perhaps? One who had forgotten or abandoned his mission to unite Europe peacefully, whereas Kaspar could have been – and may yet become – the focus of a new 'spiritualised' Europe?

* * *

It was the night of a full moon, 5th-6th April 1909, that Rudolf Steiner chose for the laying of the foundation stone of the Rosicrucian temple at Malsch – the first 'anthroposophical' building. It was located near Kaspar Hauser's birthplace – Karlsruhe, which, it will be remembered, lies on a straight line connecting it to Ansbach, Nuremberg and Karlstein, the castle of the last initiated Holy Roman Emperor, Charles IV. The Malsch building was known as 'Francis of Assisi', whom Steiner later explained had been a pupil of the super-earthly Buddha around 700 AD in the Black Sea region. Francis, of course, was later incarnate in the 13th century. His own destiny at that time portrayed the change from Mars to Mercury, as he was a warrior in his youth. That night of the 5th-6th April Rudolf Steiner spoke these words:

We want to sink the foundation stone of this temple into the womb of our Mother Earth, beneath the rays of the Full Moon shining down upon us here, surrounded by the greenness of nature enveloping the building. And just as the Moon reflects the bright light of the Sun, so do we seek to mirror the light of the divine-spiritual beings. Full of trust we turn towards our great Mother Earth, who bears us and protects us so lovingly... In pain and suffering our Mother Earth has become hardened. It is our mission to spiritualize her again, to redeem her, in that through the power of our hands we reshape her to become a spirit-filled work of art. May this stone be a first foundation stone for the redemption and transformation of our Planet Earth, and may the power of this stone multiply itself a thousandfold. When we were still resting in the bosom of the Creator, surrounded by divine powers, the all-penetrating and all-embracing Father Spirit wove within us. But we were still without consciousness, not possessing independence. For that reason we descended into matter in order to learn here to have self-consciousness. Then evil came. Then came Death. But Christ was also active within matter and helped us to overcome death, and as we now die in Christ, so do we live. We shall overcome death and through our strong powers we shall deify and spiritualise matter. So shall the power of the Healing Holy Spirit awaken within us.[166]

Is this not a picture of Kaspar Hauser's life, spoken here in the place near where he was born? Considering the immense significance of Kaspar Hauser, it may appear to some surprising that Rudolf Steiner did not say more about him beyond the few references that we have. It seems that there may be two reasons for this, one highly esoteric, the other more 'earthly.' There is a spiritual rule that secrets pertaining to the Rosicrucian work may not be spoken about for 100 years.[167] This rule was particularly apposite in this case because the direct descendant of Grand Duke Leopold of the Hochberg line, the man who supplanted Kaspar Hauser as rightful Prince of Baden in 1830, was Prince Max von Baden (1867-1929) who would become the last Chancellor of Imperial Germany at the very end of the First World War (3rd October 1918 – 9th November 1918). As described in Chapter 2[168], he was the man in high office on whom Rudolf Steiner placed his last hopes of bringing the Threefold Social Order before the world in the name of Germany, to stand as a spiritual response to the barren abstractions of Woodrow Wilson's 14 Points. Rudolf Steiner had had two conversations with Prince Max in 1918, one in Karlsruhe and one in Berlin. The Prince's freedom to represent the Threefold Social Order could not be compromised by having all kinds of things said in public about his abused ancestor Kaspar Hauser. As it was, to Rudolf Steiner's very great disappointment, Prince Max failed to present the Threefold Social Order ideas to the world and instead, agreed to an armistice on the basis of the 14 Points. Rudolf Steiner described this as an "awful spiritual capitulation." [169] But there is something else that connects Malsch with

Kaspar Hauser. Tradowsky reports that Rudolf Steiner spoke of the Karlsruhe region in relation to an area of the sinking Atlantean continent and at the dedication ceremony of the 'Francis of Assisi branch,' on 6th April 1909, Rudolf Steiner linked it again with Atlantis and spoke of how the great Sun Initiate of the Sun Oracle had "gathered a small group of people around him who were to bear the spiritual life of Atlantis into the post-Atlantean cultures..." It was expressly stated later: "The features of Old Atlantis are being repeated." [170]

What Kaspar Hauser brought from his cell and showed to his contemporaries bears witness to those primal and creative powers of childhood – openness, trust, acceptance and gratitude which enable us to "become like little children..." [171] and without which, Christ said, we would not as adults enter into the spiritual world. For a short time during his stay in Nuremberg with his friends and supporters around him, Kaspar Hauser was like the Prince in Goethe's fairy tale of *The Green Snake and The Beautiful Lily,* bringing all together at the right time, building the bridge between worlds, and he could have been such had he lived, perhaps as Prince of Baden or King of a united Germany, but as it was, he had built the bridge anyway, alone in the dark for 12 years, sustained only by the spiritual world and a single unknown, unseen human being ("the man," as he called him) who provided him only with the most basic bodily needs. During the five years in Nuremberg he built the bridge through the effect he had on people's hearts, minds and memories. A sacrifice was needed to build that bridge across the darkness of the 19th century, and through his life and death he built it well, for did he not give to us the possibility to see the Etheric Christ?

Endnotes

GA = Gesamtausgabe The Collected Works of Rudolf Steiner
(reference numbers)

1   From *Movie Magazine International*
        http://www.shoestring.org/mmi_revs/mystery_kaspar.html
2   http://www.mysteriouspeople.com/Hauser3.htm
3   From a film review at the website *strictly film school*
        http://www.filmref.com/directors/dirpages/herzog.html
4   P. Tradowsky, *Kaspar Hauser – The Struggle for the Spirit*
        (Temple Lodge, 1997), p. 281
5   Quoted in Tradowsky, pp. 275-6
6   Tradowsky, p. 280
7   Lecture of 31st Dec. 1911, in *Occult History* (Rudolf Steiner Press, 1982)
8   See R. Seddon, *Mani – His Life and Work* (Temple, Lodge, 1998)
9   See Seddon, p. 87
10 A meditative verse given by Rudolf Steiner 2nd Sept. 1923 at the founding
        meeting of the Anthroposophical Society in Great Britain
11 1928; translated as *The Ninth Century and the Holy Grail*
        (Temple Lodge, 1988)
12 Stein, p. 229
13 http://www.genealogienetz.de/reg/BAD-WUE/hist.html
14 Given in Norway in 1910 (Garber Communications, 1989)
15 Tradowsky, pp. 231-2
16 Tradowsky, p. 232
17 K. Heyer, *Kaspar Hauser and the Destiny of Middle Europe in the
        19th Century* (Perseus Verlag, 1999), untranslated, p. 274
18 For pictures, see http://www.schloss-beuggen.de/
19 J. Mayer, *Lord Stanhope – Der Gegenspieler Kaspar Hausers*
        (Urachhaus, 1988), untranslated, p. 137;
        http://www.an-netz.de/home/fam-kramer/dolch.jpg
20 Mayer, p. 264
21 Tradowsky, p. 278
22 R. Steiner, *Anthroposophical Leading Thoughts*
        (Rudolf Steiner Press, 1973), p. 213
23 2nd October 1916 "The Templars" English translation: manuscript Z156
        Rudolf Steiner House Library, London

Endnotes

24   GA 178, lecture of 25 November 1917 in *Secret Brotherhoods and the Mystery of the Human Double* (Rudolf Steiner Press, 2004)

25   GA 141, *Between Death and Rebirth* (Rudolf Steiner Press), 1975

26   http://www.kirjasto.sci.fi/schiller.htm

27   Discussed in more detail below; see pp. 138, 149 ff.

28   See Rudolf Steiner's lectures of 14th Oct.ober1917 in *The Fall of the Spirits of Darkness*, (Rudolf Steiner Press, 1993) and 17th Feb. 1918 in *The Archangel Michael – His Mission and Ours* (Anthroposophic Press, 1994)

29   GA 130, lecture of 18th December 1912, in *Esoteric Christianity and the Mission of Christian Rosenkreutz* (Rudolf Steiner Press, 1984)

30   Heyer, p. 23

31   R. Steiner, quoted in Tradowsky, p. 278

32   J. Godwin, *The Theosophical Enlightenment* (State University of New York Press, 1994), p. 80

33   Godwin, p. 81

34   Quoted in Tradowsky, p. 277

35   R. Steiner, GA 173, lecture of 9 December 1916, published in English as *The Karma of Untruthfulness Vol. 1* (Rudolf Steiner Press, 2005)

36   E. Grosse, *Das Wirken der Okkultem Logen und die Aufgabe der Mitte zwischen Ost und West*, (Verlag die Pforte, 1987), pp. 65-73

37   English translation – Rudolf Steiner Press, 1997

38   See, for example, A.C. Sutton, *Wall Street and the Bolshevik Revolution* (Arlington House, 1974)

39   For the experiment, see the statements made in 1893 by occultist C. G. Harrison, *The Transcendental Universe* (Lindisfarne Press, 1993) pp. 95-99, 173-178

40   A. C. Sutton, *America's Secret Establishment. An Introduction to the Order of Skull & Bones* (Liberty House Press, 1986)

41   Tradowsky, p. 277

42   Golden Blade magazine, 1992

43   Black Rose Books, 1999

44   Godwin, p. 164

45   Mayer, p. 94

46   *De Augmentis Scientiarum*, 1623

47   In E. Rothschild, *Language and Empire c.1800* at: http://repositories.cdlib.org/cgi/viewcontent.cgi?article=1008&context=globalfellows

48   http://41.1911encyclopedia.org/G/GE/GENTZ_FRIEDRICH_VON.htm

49   http://repositories.cdlib.org/cgi/viewcontent.cgi?article=1008&context=globalfellows

50   Mayer, p. 101

51   See note 49
52   Rothschild, loc.cit.
53   http://www.arts.gla.ac.uk/Slavonic/Czechcens.html
54   L.M. Bassani, *The Bankruptcy of the Republican School* at:
       http://www.mises.org/asc/2002/asc8-bassani.pdf
55   Rothschild, loc.cit.
56   Rothschild, loc.cit.
57   http://encyclopedia.jrank.org/GAG_GEO/GENTZ_FRIEDRICH_
       VON_1764_1832_.html
58   http://www.newadvent.org/cathen/04204a.htm
59   http://clublet.com/c/c/why?JosephDeMaistre
60   J. M. Roberts, *The Mythology of the Secret Societies*
       (Secker & Warburg, 1972), p. 297
61   http://www.umanitoba.ca/faculties/arts/history/links/maistre/
       maistrebio.html
62   http://www.newadvent.org/cathen/04034a.htm
63   See p.56
64   Gentz, Tagebücher, i. 27-8. In Rothschild, see n. 47, and Mayer, p.130
65   J. Lacouture, *The Jesuits* (Harville, 1996), p.336
66   *Lord Stanhope – The Opponent of Kaspar Hauser*
       (Urachhaus, 1988), untranslated
67   http://7.1911encyclopedia.org/C/CZ/CZARTORYSKI_ADAM_
       GEORGE_PRINCE.htm
68   http://www.celtoslavica.de/bibliothek/serbian.html
69   GA 204, *Materialism and the Task of Anthroposophy*
       (Anthroposophic Press, 1987)
70   GA 173, R. Steiner, *The Karma of Untruthfulness, Volumes 1 and 2*
       (Rudolf Steiner Press, 2005)
71   http://www.suc.org/culture/history/berlin78/congress.html?Suc_Session
       =25459c60a9646ec0f98c73c3414601b8#13
72   R. Steiner, lecture 12, 1st May 1921, quoted in *Materialism and the Task of
       Anthroposophy*
73   http://www.jewishgen.org/jcr-org/susser/thesis/thesischapternine.htm
74   J. Rae, *Life of Adam Smith* (Macmillan and Co., 1895)
75   Godwin, p. 101
76   http://www.heymannfamily.com/phpgedview/individual.php?pid
       =I12098&GEDCOM=Heymann20Feb04.GED
77   http://freemasonry.bcy.ca/textfiles/famous.html

Endnotes

78   *TIMELINE OF THE AUTHENTIC TRADITION: the foundation stone of the Antiquities of the Illuminati. Version 2.6* at: http://www.antiqillum.com/texts/tl/TLSix-009.htm

79   http://tejones.net/Unpublished_Essays/Schleiermacher.pdf

80   N. Ferguson, *The World's Banker* (Weidenfeld & Nicolson, 1998), p. 45

81   http://john-charles-herries.biography.ms/

82   http://www.danbyrnes.com.au/blackheath/thebc14.htm

83   http://www.zeit.de/2004/25/M-Rothschild Niall Ferguson, translated from the original German by TMB

84   Wilhem von Humboldt in *Prospects: the quarterly review of comparative education* – (Paris, UNESCO: International Bureau of Education), vol. XXIII, no. 3/4, 1993, pp. 613-23 http://www.ibe.unesco.org/International/Publications/ Thinkers/ThinkersPdf/humbolde.PDF

85   Count Corti, *The Rise and the Reign of the House of Rothschild Vol. I* (Victor Gollancz, 1928), p. 81

86   Corti, Vol. II, p. 619

87   http://www.antiqillum.com/texts/tl/TLSix-009.htm

88   http://www.antiqillum.com/texts/tl/TLSix-009.htm

89   See, for example, Tradowsky, 1997

90   R. Steiner, *The Archangel Michael – His Mission and Ours* (Anthroposophic Press, 1994)

91   Tradowsky, p. 278

92   1812, 1813, 1816; trans. 1929

93   http://www.gwfhegel.org/Books/CAIRD4.html

94   http://www.litencyc.com/php/speople.php?rec=true&UID=2064

95   http://www.newgenevacenter.org/biography/hegel2.htm

96   http://www.newgenevacenter.org/biography/hegel2.htm

97   http://www.hegel.net/en/eb1911.htm#333

98   GA 199, *Spiritual Science as a Foundation for Social Forms* (Anthroposophic Press), p. 153

99   GA 199, p. 156ff.

100 GA 173, lecture of 18th December 1916, in *The Karma of Untruthfulness Vol. 1* (Rudolf Steiner Press, 2005)

101 Ibid.

102 GA 174, lecture of 15th January 1917, in *The Karma of Untruthfulness Vol. 2* (Rudolf Steiner Press, 2005)

103 GA 202, *The Bridge Between Universal Spirituality and the Physical Constitution of Man* (Anthroposophic Press, 1958), p. 60

104   Liberty House Press, 1986

105   *Rudolf Steiner and Marie Steiner von Sivers, Correspondence and Documents 1901-1925.* (Anthroposophic Press, 1988)

106   R. Steiner, *Story of My Life*, ch. XXI
         (The Anthroposophical Publishing Company, 1928)

107   R.Steiner, *Vom Menschenrätsel [The Riddle of Man]*
         (Mercury Press 1990), p. 41

108   Ibid. p. 45

109   R. Steiner, *Individualism in Philosophy* (Mercury Press, 1989), p. 49

110   Steiner, *Story of My Life*, ch. XXVII

111   F. Engels, *Ludwig Feuerbach and the End of Classical German Philosophy* at:
         http://www.marxists.org/archive/marx/works/1886/ludwig-
         feuerbach/ch01.htm#013

112   http://www.marxists.org/reference/archive/hegel/index.htm

113   Steiner, *The Riddle of Man*, pp. 44-45

114   R.Steiner, *Mysticism at the Dawn of the Modern Age* at:
         http://rsarchive.org/Books/GA007/English/GA007_Intro.html

115   R.Steiner, lecture of 16th June 1910, GA 121, *The Mission of the Folk Souls
         in connection with Germanic/Scandinavian Mythology* (Garber, 1989)

116   Steiner, *The Riddle of Man*, see n. 107

117   Ibid.

118   http://www.mises.org/story/1447

119   http://byronw.www1host.com/files/FED%20Skousen%201980.pdf

120   E. Bernstein, *Ferdinand Lassalle*, ch. IX at:
         http://www.marxists.org/reference/archive/bernstein/works/
         1893/lassalle/chap09.htm

121   Bernstein, loc.cit.

122   http://gutenberg.spiegel.de/ball/krintell/krint401.htm

123   Bernstein, loc.cit.

124   See Bernstein, ch. 2

125   Libertarian Alliance Historical Notes No. 19, 1992

126   http://www.kirjasto.sci.fi/ludwig.htm

127   Heyer, p. 281

128   Heyer, p. 124

129   Tradowsky, p. 55

130   Tradowsky, ibid.

131   For its earthly reflection, see pages 108-110

132   3rd March 1925, Tradowsky, p. 281

133   Tradowsky, p. 287

134   Tradowsky, p. 57

Endnotes

135 R. Steiner, GA 185, *From Symptom to Reality in Modern History*, lecture IV (Rudolf Steiner Press, 1976)

136 17th and 19th January 1915, GA 157, *The Destinies of Individuals and of Nations* (Rudolf Steiner Press, 1987)

137 R.Steiner, GA 194, *Ideas for a New Europe* (Rudolf Steiner Press, 1992), p. 49

138 See n. 136

139 GA 121, see n. 115

140 GA 157, see n. 136

141 Tradowsky, p. 74-81

142 See K.Heyer, *Wer ist der deutsche Volksgeist? [Who is the German Folk Spirit?]* (Perseus Verlag 1990), untranslated, pp. 171 ff.

143 See *The Archangel Michael – His Mission and Ours*, pp. 61-2

144 See R. Steiner, *Occult Science – An Outline* (Rudolf Steiner Press, 1969), ch. 4

145 See n. 115 Lecture 11

146 S.O. Prokofieff, *The Cycle of the Year as a Path of Initiation* (Temple Lodge Press 1991), p. 276

147 Tradowsky, p. 217

148 GA 93a, *Foundations of Esotericism*, Berlin, 28th October 1905, (Rudolf Steiner Press, 1983)

149 Beyond Words Publishing, 2004

150 P.Tradowsky, *Aufs neue nach so langer Frist... [Kaspar Hauser in the Spiritual Struggle of the Present]* Verlag am Goetheanum, 1998, untranslated

151 Ibid.

152 *Correspondence and Documents*, pp. 16-17

153 I am indebted to the historian Dr. Markus Osterrieder of Munich for this information about Dmitri's education, about the Polish Brethren and the medallion – TMB

154 GA 130, 18th December 1912, *Esoteric Christianity and the Mission of Christian Rosenkreutz* (Rudolf Steiner Press, 1984

155 Tradowsky, *Aufs neue nach so langer Frist...*, p. 30

156 See for example her groundbreaking book *The Rosicrucian Enlightenment* (Routledge & Kegan Paul, 1972)

157 See *The Archangel Michael – His Mission and Ours*

158 2nd May 1913, *The Archangel Michael – His Mission and Ours*

159 See lecture 1 in R.Steiner, *The Reappearance of Christ in the Etheric* (Anthroposophic Press, 1983)
    Steiner first referred to the Etheric Reappearance of Christ in a lecture in Stockholm on 12th January 1910, but the texts of the lectures given in Stockholm that winter do not survive.

160 See n. 158
161 Tradowsky, p. 277
162 R.Steiner GA 131, *From Jesus to Christ* (Rudolf Steiner Press, 2005)
163 K. Heyer, *Kaspar Hauser and ...* p. 241 – translated by TMB
164 Tradowsky, p. 68-9
165 http://en.wikipedia.org/wiki/Kaspar_Hauser
166 GA 284, *Mystic Seals and Columns*, (Health Research Books, 1969)
167 27th September 1911. See n. 154
168 See pp. 25-27
169 Tradowsky, p. 232
170 Tradowsky, p. 221-2
171 Matthew 18:3

Index

A

Africa 153
Alemanni 17
Alsace 17
Alsace-Lorraine 16, 19
American Civil War 46, 129
American Revolution 44, 70, 71, 74, 91
Anacalypsis 54
Ancient and Accepted Scottish Rite of
  Freemasonry 91
Anglo-Saxons 140, 141
Ansbach 17, 21, 64, 73, 94, 108, 126,
  165
Anthroposophy 10, 37, 39, 94, 95,
  125, 136
Apostles 28
Arabia 146
Archai 145
Aries 49
Aristotelianism 94
Asia 46, 111, 112, 153
Atlantis 11, 17, 30, 40, 41, 111, 132,
  146, 147, 167
Ausgleich 51, 129
Australia 141
Austria 24, 34, 50, 58, 66, 78, 80, 81,
  93, 129, 162
Austria-Hungary 51, 61, 129
Austro-Prussian War 34, 51

B

Baden 11, 16, 17, 19, 22, 23, 24, 25,
  26, 30, 33, 34, 50, 62, 63, 77, 99, 113,
  127, 128, 132, 148, 160, 163, 166
Baden-Baden 22
Baden-Durlach 22

Baden-Württemberg 17
Baha'i 15
Balkans 80, 81, 130
Baltic 28
Basel (Basle) 19, 20
Bavaria 21, 28, 30, 32, 34, 50, 63, 113,
  120, 122, 127, 128, 129, 160
Bayreuth 33, 129
Belgium 17
Benares 152
Benedictines 151
Berlin 42, 71, 77, 97, 108, 127, 131,
  142, 145
Berlin Wall 26, 166
Berne 97
Beuggen 21, 26, 27, 131
Bible 11, 133, 151
Black Forest 17
Black Sea 106, 165
Bohemian Brothers 150
Bolshevism 61
Bosnia(-Herzegovina) 78, 81
Bosphorus 78
Brandenburg 122
Breslau 76
Britain 15, 24, 40, 46, 50, 56, 61, 64, 66,
  71, 79, 100, 119, 123, 128, 142, 162
British Empire 46, 71, 127, 139, 141
Buddhism 146, 152
Burgundy 17, 19

C

Cabbalah 53, 84, 85
Canada 141
Capital 60
Candlewax Square 30, 112, 155

Caribbean 26
Carlsbad Decrees 125
Carthage 69
(Roman) Catholic Church 74, 81,
    144, 150
Caucasus 112
Central Europe 31, 32, 34, 35, 36, 50,
    56, 60, 61, 80, 81, 92, 95, 105, 110,
    111, 127, 129, 137, 146, 150, 155, 164
Chaldeans 52, 53
Charleston 91
Chartist movement 128
Chartres 94
Chevening, Kent 139
China 46, 47, 50, 152, 155
Christian Community, the 12
Christianity 12, 18, 33, 53, 146, 147,
    152
Church of England 91
Colchis 12
Communist League 113
Concept of Dread (Kierkegaard) 109
Concordat 73, 74
Confessio Fraternitatis 152
Congress of Berlin 130
Congress (USA) 25
Congress of Vienna 28, 30, 69
Consciousness Soul 35, 136, 137, 142,
    151, 156, 159
Constance 20
Constantine 20
Constantinople 18, 19, 36, 78, 127
Corfu 78
Corsica 49
Cosmic Cultus 37, 94, 103, 125, 137
Cracow 150
Crimean War 50, 128
Crusade(s) 27
Culdees 53
Cygnus 149

D
Damascus 157
Danzig 78
Dardanelles 78
Deism 42, 53, 59, 74
Declaration of Independence (USA)
    42
Denmark 129
Der Spiegel 163
Dominicans 54
Dornach 17, 20, 136
Dresden 23
Druids 53

E
East India Company 46, 88, 135
Egypt 85
Eightfold Path, the 152
Elbe 91
Emulation Lodge 86
End of History and the Last Man, the
    (Fukuyama) 106
Essence of Christianity, the
    (Feuerbach) 108
England 20, 60, 61, 66, 67, 69, 78, 85,
    86, 93, 138, 139, 151
Elector(s) 20
Etheric Christ, the 136, 142, 156, 157,
    167
Ethiopia 153
Europe 12, 14, 16, 17, 18, 20, 28, 30,
    32, 38, 49, 58, 112, 113, 153, 155,
    159, 161
European Parliament 18
F
Factory Acts 46, 127
Fall, the 47
Fama Fraternitas 152
*Fairy Tale of the Green Snake
and the Beautiful Lily* 95, 161, 167

First Goetheanum 10, 14
First Scientific Lecture Course 41
First World War 30, 37, 56, 104, 166
Foreign Office (London) 72
Forensic Science Service, Birmingham 163
France 16, 18, 20, 22, 50, 56, 57, 58, 61, 67, 69, 74, 78, 79, 92, 100, 119, 128, 130, 138, 139
Franciscans 47, 54
Franco-Prussian War 130
Frankfurt 23, 33, 35, 52, 83, 86, 87, 97
Franks 12, 140
Freemasonry 27, 52, 53, 54, 56, 57, 58, 59, 60, 62, 66, 75, 78, 79, 81
Freiburg 20, 21
French Revolution 44, 71, 73, 74, 86, 89, 90, 92, 100, 136

G
Gabriel, the Age of 100, 134, 140, 142, 156
Gemini 42
Genesis 11
Georgia 12
German Confederation 93
Germany 13, 16, 17, 18, 19, 20, 21, 23, 24, 25, 26, 27, 30, 32, 33, 35, 50, 61, 64, 67, 73, 74, 77, 78, 86, 88, 91, 92, 108, 113, 115, 118, 123, 139, 146, 147, 155, 159, 161, 162, 166, 167
Glorious Revolution (1688) 123
Golden Bull 20, 155
Golden Fleece, Order of 80
Golgotha 154, 156, 164
Göttingen University 84
Grail 13, 18, 20, 32, 33, 35, 38, 95, 106, 122, 123, 140, 141, 144
Grand Orient 85, 87
Great Britain 24, 118

Great Comet of 1811 125
Great Crash 44
Great Reform Bill (1832) 127
Great Synagogue 83
Gulf Crisis 30
Gulf of Mexico 91
Gulf War 30

H
Habsburg 20, 79, 81, 124, 129
hakenkreuz 30
Halley's Comet 30, 37
Hambacher Fest 23, 127
Hampton Court Conference 151
Hanover 84
Hardtwald Forest 22
Hegelianism 108, 113
Heidelberg 17, 28, 97
Hibernian Mysteries 17, 18
Hindu(s) 40
Hohenstaufen 20
Hohenzollern 20, 116, 161
Holland 17, 60
Holy Lance 20
Holy Roman Emperor 14, 19, 20, 164
Holy Roman Empire 19, 20, 21, 50, 110
Holy Spirit 28
Hundred Years' War, the 138

I
Iberia 28
Illuminati 75, 77, 80, 90, 160
Imagination 43, 45, 95
Industrial Revolution 15, 37, 40
Ingolstadt 160
Inquisition, the 44
Intellectual-Mind Soul 35, 128
Inspiration 43, 45

Institute for Forensic Medicine,
   University of Münster 163
Intuition 43, 45
Ionian islands 78
Islam 146
Israel 54, 146, 147, 155
Italy 17, 20, 73, 84

J
Japan 15, 152
Japanese Buddhism 47, 54
Jena 97
Jesuitism 60, 76
Jesuits 45, 47, 51, 56, 56, 57, 62, 63,
   66, 74, 75, 78, 79, 81, 93, 150, 160
Jewish Daily Post 82
Jolly Roger 27
Judengasse 88
July Revolution (1830) 127
Jupiter 28, 129, 149

K
Kali Yuga 39, 40, 157
Karlsruhe 16, 17, 18, 22, 26, 156, 165,
   167
Karlstejn 17, 165
Kassel 152
Katrina 92
*Knowledge of the Higher Worlds and
   How It Is Achieved* 153
Königsberg 66, 90
Korea 152
Kristallnacht 26

L
Laufenburg 26, 73
Leipzig 89
Lemuria 40, 41, 47, 49
Libertarian Alliance 118
Liegnitz 13

Life Spirit 43, 129
Ljubljana 70
Lombards 141
London 63, 71, 72, 73, 83, 85, 86,
   156, 157
Lotharingia (Lorraine) 17, 18
Louisiana Purchase 91, 92

M
Malsch 165, 166
Marne, Battle of 60
Mediterranean 28, 49
Michael, the Age of 37, 39, 100, 103,
   110, 140, 142
Michaelmas 17
Magi 13, 44, 45, 46
Manchester 83
Manichaeism 12, 14, 134, 135, 136
Mannheim 23, 28
Marmora, Sea of 78
Mars 11, 13, 47, 49, 50, 51, 128, 129,
   137, 140, 151, 152, 153, 154, 155,
   156, 164, 165
Mars-Mercury 49, 147
Marxism 44
Mercury 49, 50, 125, 145, 147, 152,
   153, 154, 164, 165,
Mises Institute 71, 114
Misraim, Rite of 90
Mississippi 91, 92
Montenegro 78
Moon 30, 125, 130, 165
Moon Node 38, 39, 40, 44, 126, 129
Mostar 78
Munich 26, 63, 160
Mysteries, pre-Christian 32

Index

N

Nain 12, 13
Naometria 149
Naros (Neros) Cycle 52, 54, 56
Nascent Dawn Lodge 87
Nazis 26, 155
Nazism 118
Neptune 37, 43, 45, 50, 130
Neuschwanstein Castle 33, 120, 122, 129
Newgate Prison 84
New Orleans 92
New Testament 44
New York 130
New Zealand 141
Nichiren sect (of Buddhism) 47, 54
Niebelungs 12, 122
Niebelungenlied 20
Norman Conquest 65
Normans 37
North America 141, 151
Nuremberg 17, 20, 21, 22, 28, 30, 64, 93, 97, 102, 106, 108, 113, 125, 126, 127, 150, 155, 160, 161, 165, 167
Nuremberg Royal Grammar School 97

O

Objective Logic (Hegel) 97
Odilienberg 17, 18
Ophiuchus 49
Opium Wars 44, 46, 129
Order of the Swan 122
Ottoman Empire 80, 127

P

Palatinate 17, 23, 24, 28, 34, 50, 63, 118, 127
Palestine 18, 49, 128
Pan-Slavism 80, 81
Papacy 27, 57, 81

Paris 79, 81, 92, 127, 130
Pentecost 28
Persia 15
Peterloo Massacre 125
Pforzheim 26
Phenomenology of Spirit/Mind (Hegel) 101
Philosophy of Revelation from the Right (Schelling) 109
Philosophy of Spiritual Activity (Steiner) 103, 125, 131
Piedmont & Sardinia, Kingdom of 77, 79
Pilsach 28, 113, 125, 135, 160
Pluto 43, 45, 131
Poland 13, 23, 58, 137, 150
Polish Brethren 150
Portugal 57
Portsmouth 63
Prague 17
Project for a New American Century 106
Prussia 24, 34, 50, 57, 58, 76, 77, 78, 81, 93, 113, 115, 119, 128, 129, 130, 161
Pure Land School (Buddhist) 47

R

Ragusa 78
Reformation 22
Regensburg 20
Reichstag 34
Rheinfelden 26
Rhine 17, 18, 26, 73
Rhineland 21
Riddle of Man (Steiner) 105, 112
Rocky Mountains 91
Rome 139
Romantics 45, 70

Rosicrucianism 12, 13, 52, 106, 134,
  137, 146, 147, 148, 152, 155, 165
Royal Society 52
Russia 10, 23, 28, 50, 57, 58, 60, 61,
  74, 76, 77, 78, 79, 80, 81, 91, 119,
  125, 137, 138, 150, 159
Russian Civil War 61
Ruthenia 150

S
Saturn 42, 43, 45, 129, 149
Savoy 77
Saxony 21, 23
Scandinavia 146
Science of Logic (Hegel) 97, 102, 103
Schreinerei 10
Schönbrunn Palace 50
Scottish Rite (Masonry) 75
Second Coming 44, 136, 142
Serbia 79, 80
Serpentarius 149
Seven Years' War 56
Sicily 63
Skull and Bones 27, 62, 106
Social Democratic Party (SPD) 115
Solomon, Temple of 84
South Africa 141
Spain 57
Spiritland 42, 43, 45
Spirit Man 43, 129
Spirit Self 43, 129
Spirits of Form 47
Spiritualism 44
Sponheim 28, 63
SS, the 27
Stanford University 106
St Gumbertus church 122, 126
St Petersburg 77, 78, 81
St Helena 50
Strasbourg 18

Stuttgart 17, 95, 145, 147
Subjective Logic (Hegel) 97
Suevii 17, 19
Sun 30, 37, 43, 125, 126, 167
Sun Oracle 12, 17, 30
Swabia 19, 20, 27
Swabian League 20, 21
Swan Knight(s) 122, 126
Switzerland 17, 19

T
Tallow Square 30
Templar(s) 27, 52, 151
Tenrikyo 15
Testament of Peter the Great 58, 60
Teutonic Knights 27
Theosophy (R.Steiner) 42, 43
Theosophical Society 39, 130, 131
The Robbers 45
Third Reich, the 141, 144
Thirty Years' War 64, 128, 130
Threefold Social Order 24, 25, 154,
  166
Tibet 152
Totenkopf 27
Triple Entente 119
Tübingen 97, 99
Tudor dynasty 138
Tugendbund 66, 90
Turin 77

U
Ukraine 150
Unitarianism 53
United Grand Lodge 52
United States 15, 42, 44, 46, 61, 66,
  74, 91, 92, 114, 164
Unschlittplatz 30
Uranus 41, 42, 43, 44, 45, 63, 65, 93,
  124, 130

Index

V

Vatican 73, 74
Venus 126
Verona, Congress of 72
Versailles 110, 130
Vienna 50, 63, 64, 66, 72, 73, 77, 79
Visigoths 141
Vistula 78
Volhynia 150
Voyager 2 space probe 42

W

Wallachia 78
War in Heaven 37, 46, 100, 109, 113,
    128, 130, 133
Waterloo 90
Wealth of Nations 67, 84
Weimar Republic 25, 107
World War II 64
Worms 21
Württemberg 21

Y

Yale University 27, 106
Yorktown 44

Z

Zähringen 11, 19, 126
Zen (Buddhism) 54
Zodiac 43, 45
Zoroastrianism 152

Index of Names

A

Adams, John Quincy 71
Adhemar, Countess d' 130
Ahriman 14, 93, 97, 103, 104, 128,135
Ahura-Mazdao 14
Albert of Saxe-Coburg, Prince
   Consort, 24, 118, 119, 123, 128
Alexander I, Czar of Russia 77, 78, 79
Alexander the Great 18
Andreae, Johann Valentin 149, 150
Arc, Joan of 138, 139
Archiati, Pietro, 38
Aristotle 18
Arnim, Bettina von 99
Attila 123
Augustus Frederick,
   the Duke of Sussex 52, 53, 54, 57,
   74, 78, 82, 83, 84, 86, 93

B

Babbage, Charles 65
Bach J.S., 136
Bacon, Francis 65, 80, 101
Baden, Grand Duke Karl of 11, 23,
   77, 99, 160 see Karl
Baden, Luisa von 77
Baden, Max von 24, 25, 26, 166
   see Max
Bakunin, Mikhail 109
Bapst, Edmond 26
Barère, Bertrand 69
Baring, Alexander 92
Barmakid, Jafar 18
Barruel, Abbé 75
Basilii, Johannis 150
Bassani, Luigi Marco 71

Bavaria, King Ludwig I of 28
Beauharnais, Stephanie de,
   see Stephanie
Bédarride, Michel 91
Beethoven, Ludwig van 98, 136
Binder, Mayor 94
Bismarck, Otto von 33, 34, 51, 113,
   114, 115, 116, 118, 119, 120, 125,
   129, 130, 131, 139, 161, 162
Blavatsky, Helena P. 130
Blochmann, Kasper Ernst 127
Boehme, Jacob 95, 111
Bonaparte, see Napoleon
Brentano, Clemens 99
Brockdorff, Count von 131
Brockdorff, Countess von 131
Brougham, Lord Henry 80
Bruce, Jacob 60
Bruce, Robert the 65
Bruckner, Anton 124
Bruno S 9
Buddha, Gautama 12, 47, 49, 50, 54,
   145, 146, 151, 152, 153, 154, 155,
   156, 162, 165
Bulwer-Lytton, Sir Edward 85, 116
Burke, Edmund 66, 71
Bush, George W. 27, 62, 106
Bush, Prescott 106
Byron, Lord 65

C

Cagliostro 85
Cambridge, Duke of 83
Caspar (one of the Magi) 13
Castlereagh, Lord Robert Stewart,
   Viscount 69

Catherine the Great of Russia 57, 76

Charlemagne, Holy Roman Emperor
17, 19, 51, 164

Charles IV, Holy Roman Emperor 14,
17, 20, 165

Charles the Bald, King of the Franks 17

Christ, Jesus 13, 38, 60, 101, 133, 134,
135, 136, 142, 146, 147, 148, 149,
150, 151, 152, 153, 154, 156, 157,
159, 161, 162, 163, 164, 166, 167

Choiseul, Duc de 56

Clarence, Duke of 84

Clausewitz, Carl von 99

Clement XIV, Pope 57, 76

Clovis 74

Coleridge, Samuel T. 45, 70

Comte, Auguste 109

Confucius 54

Conradin, Duke of Swabia 27

Cumberland, Duke of 83

Cyril, (Orthodox missionary) 61

Cyrus the Great, King of Persia 54

Czartoryski, Prince Adam Jerzy 53,
77, 78, 79, 80, 81

Czartoryski, Prince 79

D

Dalbonne, Anna 28

Dalcho, Dr. Frederick 91

Daumer, Georg Friedrich, Professor
49, 94, 97, 126, 133, 147

Dee, Dr. John 155

Derby, Lord Edward Smith-Stanley,
14th Earl of 88

D'Hauterive, Alexandre 69, 72

Disraeli, Benjamin 88, 116, 130

D'Ivernois, Francois 67

Demetrius 132

Dmitri, Czarist pretender 10, 45, 138,
150

E

Ebert, Friedrich 25

Eckhartshausen, Karl 75

Eden, William, Lord Auckland 72

Edward Albert, Prince of Wales,
later King Edward VII 24

Edward III, King of England 138

Edward IV, King of England 138

Edward VII, King of Great Britain
24, 119

Eichhorn, Karl Friedrich 99

Elijah 54

Elizabeth I, Queen of England 140

Elizabeth Stuart, Princess, daughter of
King James I 17, 24, 118, 137, 153

Eliza von Moltke 60

Emoto, Masaru 148

Engels, Friedrich 108, 109, 114

Enghien, duc d' 78

Erskine, Robert 60

Eschenbach, Wolfram von 20

F

Falk, Samuel 85, 86

Faust 136

Ferdinand, (character in
Shakespeare's *The Tempest*) 137

Ferguson, Niall 87, 89

Feuerbach, Anselm von, Court
President 94, 108, 109, 126, 133,
136, 159, 163

Feuerbach, Henriette 136

Feuerbach, Ludwig von 108, 118

Fichte, Johann Gottlieb 98, 111

Fierifis, (character in *Parzival* by
Wolfram von Eschenbach), 13

Forster-Nietzsche, Elizabeth 131

Francis of Assisi, Saint 165

Francis I, Emperor of Austria 70

Franklin, Benjamin 40, 41, 42

Franz Josef, Emperor of Austria
(later Austria-Hungary) 124
Frederick I, Duke of Baden 24
Frederick III, Emperor of Germany
24, 119
Frederick V, Elector of the Palatinate
17, 24, 118, 137,152
Frederick the Great of Prussia 57, 76
Friedrich, Duke of Swabia 27
Frederick I Barbarossa, Holy Roman
Emperor 20, 23
Frederick II, Holy Roman Emperor
20, 23
Friedrich, Caspar David 99
Friedrich II, Prince of Brandenburg
122
Friedrich Wilhelm IV, King of Prussia
33, 113, 128,
Fuhrmann, Pastor 94, 122, 126, 127,
135
Fukuyama, Francis 106

G
Gabriel, Archangel 36, 37, 100, 134,
142, 156, 159
Galvani 40, 41, 63
Garlike, Benjamin 67
Gentz, Friedrich von 53, 63, 64, 66,
67, 69, 70, 71, 72, 73, 76, 77, 81, 88,
89, 90, 93
George III, King of England 52, 72,
82, 86
Gerasanin, Illija 80, 81
Germain, Count St 56, 57, 130, 136
Gneisenau, August von 98
Goderich, Lord 88
Goethe, Johann Wolfgang 18, 23, 32,
38, 51, 72, 93, 95, 98, 102, 126, 135,
136, 143, 155, 161, 164, 167
Goldsmid, Aaron 86

Goldsmid, Abraham 82, 83, 86
Goldsmid, Benjamin 86
Gordon, Lord George 84
Grenville, Louisa, Baroness 72
Grenville, William Wyndham, Lord
67, 72
Grey, Charles, 2nd Earl 80
Griesenbeck, Mayor Karl von 28, 30
Grimm, Jakob 99
Grimm, Wilhelm 99

H
Habsburg family 20
Hamerling, Robert 112
Hamilton, Emma 84
Hamilton, William, Sir 84
Harun al-Rashid 18
Hart, Solomon 84
Hastings, Warren 78
Hatzfeld, Countess Sophie von 116
Haydn, Joseph 98
Hecker, F. 23
Hegel, Georg Wilhelm Friedrich 23,
32, 62, 95, 97, 98, 99, 100, 101, 103,
104, 105, 106, 107, 108, 109, 110,
111, 113, 117, 126
Heine, Heinrich 99
Hennenhofer, Major Johann Heinrich
David von 62
Henry I, King of Germany 19
Henry III, King of England 65
Henry VIII, King of England 139, 140
Heraclitus 54, 113, 117
Herder, Johann Gottfried 32, 38, 95,
98
Herries-Farquhar (bank) 89
Herries, John Charles 72, 88, 89
Herschel, William 41, 63
Herz, Marcus, Dr. 90
Herz, Henriette 90

184

Herzog, Werner 9
Heyer, Karl 14, 26, 145, 146
Hickel, Joseph Lt., 62, 63
Higgins, Godfrey 52, 53
Hiltel, Andreas 94, 133
Hirschell, Rabbi 83
Hitler, Adolf 21, 30, 31, 44, 47, 64,
    127, 131, 136, 141, 162
Hochberg, Countess Luise von 24,
    26, 62, 63, 126
Hoffman, E.T.A. 99
Hohenstaufen family 20
Hohenzollern family 20
Hölderlin, Friedrich 32, 38, 95, 97,
    98, 99
Humboldt, Alexander von 98
Huns 123
Hutten 117

J
Jackson, Sir Francis 77
James I, King of England & VI of
    Scotland 17, 118, 138, 139, 151
Jefferson, Thomas 74, 92
Jesus, see Christ

K
Kant, Immanuel 66, 90, 98, 100
Karl of Baden, Grand Duke 19, 50,
    132 see Baden, Grand Duke Karl of
Karl Friedrich, Grand Duke of Baden
    22, 24
Karl Wilhelm, Duke of Baden 22
Kent, Duke of 86
Kepler, Johannes 49, 102, 149
Kerner, Justinus 21
Kierkegaard, Soren 109
Kleist, Bernd, Heinrich Wilhelm von
    99
Klopstock, Friedrich Gottlieb 98

Kojève, Alexandre 106
Kühn, Hans 25
Kukiel, Marian 79

L
Lassalle, Ferdinand 33, 34, 113, 114,
    115, 116, 118, 120, 129, 161, 162
Lavagna, Count 117
Lazarus–John 14
Leeson, Nick 92
Lemennais, Hughes de 75
Lenin, Vladimir Ilyich 130
Leo III, Pope 19
Leopold, Grand Duke of Baden 62,
    126, 166
Lessing, Gotthold Ephraim 98
Limburger, Baron 89
Lincoln, Abraham 114
Locke, John 80, 81
Lodge, Sir Oliver 104, 105
Lohengrin 120
Longinus 20
Lothar, Holy Roman Emperor,
    grandson of Charlemagne 17
Louis XIV, King of France 22, 130
Louis XV, King of France 56
Louis XVIII, King of France 69
Louis-Phillippe, Duke d'Orleans 85
Louis-Phillippe, King of France 86
Louis the Pious, Holy Roman
    Emperor, son of Charlemagne 17
Lovelace, Ada Lady 65
Ludwig I, Crown Prince and King of
    Bavaria, 30, 34, 50, 63, 113, 129
Ludwig II, King of Bavaria 32, 34, 118,
    120, 122, 126, 127, 128, 129, 130
Ludwig, Grand Duke of Baden 62,
    63, 126
Ludwig, King of the Germans 17

M

Macauley 70

Maier, Michael 150

Mahon, Viscount 64

Maistre, Count Joseph de 74, 75, 76, 77, 79, 80, 81

Mani 12, 13, 106, 107, 134, 152

Marbois, Barbé 92

Marks, Paul 118

Marx, Karl 60, 61, 114

Masson, Jeffrey Moussaieff 9

Maximilian, Emperor of Mexico 129

Max, Prince von Baden 24, see Baden, Max von

Mayer, Johannes 77

McCullough, E.E 64

Medinger, Astrid von 163

Melchizedek 54

Mendelssohn, Moses 90

Mephistopheles 141

Methodius, (Orthodox missionary) 61

Metternich, Clemens von, Prince and Chancellor of Austria 24, 50, 63, 64, 67, 70, 72, 79, 80, 81, 82, 90, 93, 125, 127, 162, 164

Metternich, Franz Georg Karl von 80

Meyer, Johann 62, 63

Meyer, Thomas 60, 73, 108, 126

Michael, Archangel 37, 94, 100, 102, 103, 122, 128, 130, 140, 142, 145, 154

Mill, John Stuart 109

Mirabeau, Honoré Gabriel Riqueti, Comte de 75

Miranda, (character in Shakespeare's *The Tempest*) 137

Mises, Ludwig von 114, 118

Mitchell, Colonel John 91

Mohammed, the Prophet 54

Moltke, General Helmuth von 60, 61

Mozart, Wolfgang Amadeus 98

Müller, Adam 70, 98

N

Nain, Young Man/Youth of 12, 13

Nakayama, Miki 15

Napoleon I (Bonaparte), Emperor of the French 11, 12, 19, 27, 30, 31, 49, 51, 58, 60, 64, 65, 66, 69, 72, 73, 74, 82, 89, 90, 92, 93, 105, 125, 135, 136, 138, 159, 164, 165

Napoleon II, King of Rome and Duke of Reichstadt 50, 165

Napoleon III, Emperor of the French 50

Nelson, Lord Horatio 84, 86

Neuffer 107

Newton, Sir Isaac 102

Nicholas I, Pope 61

Nietzsche, Friedrich 33, 34, 125, 130, 131, 162, 164

Noah 54

Nostradamus 16

Novalis 99

O

Odile, Saint 18

Odin 145, 146, 152

Ostrogski, Janusz 150

P

Palmerston, Lord Henry Temple, 3rd Viscount 80

Parenti, Michael 91

Parsifal 13, 106, 120, 122, 141

Paul, Saint 157

Peel, Sir Robert 88, 115

Perceval, Spencer 88

Pestalozzi, Johann Heinrich 28

Peter I the Great, Czar of Russia 58, 60

Pitt the Younger, William 64, 71, 77, 86, 138
Pius VII, Pope 57
Plotinus 111
Polzer-Holditz, Ludwig 10, 12, 32, 56, 93, 106, 122, 160
Preu, Dr 94
Prince of Wales, the, later King George IV, 85
Proclus 111
Prokofieff, Sergei O. 146
Przypkowski family 150
Pushkin, Aleksandr 60
Pythagoras 54

R
Racowitza, Count von 161
Reichstadt, Duke of 164
Richard III, King of England 138
Robespierre, Maximilien 58, 74
Rosenkreutz, Christian 12, 13, 14, 20, 56, 107, 130, 134, 149, 151, 152, 157
Rothschild family 135
Rothschild, Mayer Armschel 87, 88, 89, 90
Rothschild, Nathan Mayer 53, 82, 83, 86, 88, 89, 90, 93
Rudolf I, King of Burgundy 19
Rurik, Ivan IV, 'the Terrible,' Czar of Russia 150

S
Salisbury, Lord 130, 162
Samael, archangel 13, 151
Scharnhorst, Gerhard von 98
Schelling, Friedrich Wilhelm Joseph von 97, 98, 99, 109, 111
Schiller, Friedrich 32, 38, 45, 95, 98, 116, 117, 136, 138, 155, 161, 164
Schinkel, Karl Friedrich 99

Schlegel, August Wilhelm von 98
Schlegel, Karl Wilhelm Friedrich von 70, 99
Schleiermacher, Friedrich Daniel Ernst 98
Schopenhauer, Arthur 99, 109
Schröer, Karl Julius 125
Schubert, Franz 99
Shakespeare, William 144, 149
Sickingen, Franz von 117
Siegfried 122
Skythianos 12
Smith, Adam 67, 84
Sophie, Grand Duchess of Baden 62
Spittler, Christian Friedrich 28
Stalin, Josef 44, 47
Stanhope, Philip Henry, 4th Earl of 62, 63, 64, 65, 71, 72, 73, 77, 80, 85, 108, 116, 118, 125, 126, 138, 139, 157, 161, 163
Stein, Walter Johannes 18
Steiner, Rudolf 10, 11, 12, 13, 14, 15, 17, 18, 23, 24, 25, 32, 37, 38, 39, 41, 42, 45, 46, 47, 49, 50, 56, 57, 58, 60, 63, 66, 73, 76, 80, 94, 103, 104, 105, 106, 107, 108, 110, 112, 122, 125, 129, 131, 132, 134, 136, 137, 138, 139, 140, 141, 142, 143, 144, 145, 146, 147, 149, 152, 153, 155, 156, 157, 159, 160, 161, 165, 166, 167
Stephanie, Grand Duchess of Baden 11, 19, 23, 50, 99, 132, 163
see Beauharnais
Strassburg, Gottfried von 20
Struve, G. 23
Studion, Simon 149
Sucher, Willi 43
Sutton, Prof. Anthony C. 62, 106
Swedenborg, Emanuel 85
Szmalc, Walenty 150

T
Talleyrand, Charles Maurice, Prince de Benevente 69
Tassoni, Baron 91
Tennyson, Alfred, Lord 123
Teut 112
Tieck, Ludwig 99
Tradowsky, Peter 11, 64, 65, 124, 136, 142, 144, 147, 148, 149, 151, 152, 153, 154, 157, 159, 162, 167
Trotsky, Leon 61, 130
Tucher, Gottlieb, Baron von 94, 97, 108, 126, 133
Tucher, Marie von 97, 118
Twardochlebus, Matthias 150

U
Uhland, Ludwig 99

V
Victoria, Princess of England 24, 119
Victoria, Queen 24, 118, 128
Vidar, Archangel 146
Virgin Mary 122
Vogelweide, Walther von der 20
Volta, Alessandro 41
Voltaire 58

W
Wagner, Richard 32, 33, 34, 118, 120, 122, 127, 129, 130, 141
Wassermann, Jakob 107
Weber, Carl Maria von 99
Weishaupt, Adam 80, 160
Wellington, Duke of 88
Wilhelm I, Crown Prince of Prussia and then Emperor of Germany 24, 130, 161
Wilhelm II, Emperor of Germany 24, 61, 119, 125

William III, King of England 123
William IX, Elector of Hesse-Cassel 90
Wilson, Woodrow, US President 24, 25, 79, 166
Wotan 145, 146, 152

Y
Yahya Barmakid 18
Yates, Frances 155
York, Duke of 84

Z
Zähringen, Karl von 11, 20
Zavadovsky, Peter Vasilevich 78
Zeller, Christian Heinrich 28
Zevi, Sabbatai 85
Zoroaster 12